THE
DOMÍNGUEZ-ESCALANTE
JOURNAL

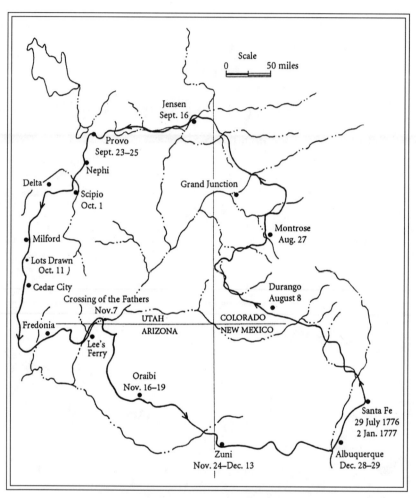

Scale

0   50 miles

Jensen
Sept. 16

Provo
Sept. 23–25

Nephi

Delta

Scipio
Oct. 1

Grand Junction

Montrose
Aug. 27

Milford

Lots Drawn
Oct. 11

Durango
August 8

Cedar City

Crossing of the Fathers
Nov.7

UTAH   COLORADO

Fredonia

ARIZONA   NEW MEXICO

Lee's
Ferry

Oraibi
Nov. 16–19

Santa Fe
29 July 1776
2 Jan. 1777

Zuni
Nov. 24–Dec. 13

Albuquerque
Dec. 28–29

DOMÍNGUEZ–ESCALANTE ROUTE, 1776

THE
DOMÍNGUEZ-ESCALANTE
JOURNAL

THEIR EXPEDITION THROUGH COLORADO, UTAH, ARIZONA, AND NEW MEXICO IN 1776

Translated by Fray Angelico Chavez

Edited by Ted J. Warner

Foreword by Robert Himmerich y Valencia

University of Utah Press
Salt Lake City

Published by special arrangement with the Utah State Historical Society

∞ Printed on acid-free paper

The University of Utah Press edition of *The Domínguez-Escalante Journal* presents the complete English-language text originally published by Brigham Young University Press, 1976. The 1995 edition contains slight modifications in the translation and greater accuracy in several of the geographic coordinates mentioned in the notes. Changes were made in consultation with Robert Himmerich y Valencia of the University of New Mexico.

Map on p. ii adapted from map in *Utah's History*, Richard D. Poll, ed. 1978. Courtesy of Utah State University Press.

Maps accompanying the journal are details from map from *Pageant in the Wilderness: The Story of the Escalante Expedition to the Interior Basin, 1776*, by Herbert E. Bolton. Salt Lake City: Utah State Historical Society, 1951.

Book design by Richard Firmage

Cover illustration from Map of Domínguez-Escalante Expedition by Don Bernardo de Miera y Pacheco, 1778. Miera map courtesy of Utah State Historical Society.

LIBRARY OF CONGRESS CATALOGING-IN-PUBLICATION DATA

Vélez de Escalante, Silvestre, d. 1792.
    [Diaro y derrotero. English]
    The Domínguez-Escalante journal : their expedition through
Colorado, Utah, Arizona, and New Mexico in 1776 / translated by
Angelico Chavez ; edited by Ted J. Warner ; foreword by
Robert Himmerich y Valencia.
       p.   cm.
    Includes bibliographical references.
    ISBN 0-87480-447-7 — ISBN 0-87480-448-5 (pbk.)
    1. Domínguez-Escalante Expedition (1776)—Personal narratives.
2. Vélez de Escalante, Silvestre, d. 1792—Diaries.   3. Domínguez,
Francisco Atanasio, fl. 1776—Diaries.   I. Warner, Ted J.   II. Title.
F799.V4413   1995   94-34187
978.9'02'092—dc20

CONTENTS

✠

FOREWORD

Bicentennial fever was upon the land in 1976, spawning a great out-pouring of celebratory writing. One of the more valuable works of scholarship set to type was this volume. Fray Angelico Chavez's translation and Ted J. Warner's editing of *The Domínguez-Escalante Journal* presented the report of a most remarkable trip in 1776 through part of the Rocky Mountains, across the eastern reaches of the Great Basin, and over the Colorado Plateau. The expedition failed in its mission to map a route from Santa Fe, New Mexico to Monterey, Alta California, but nonetheless was successful in providing a detailed inventory of a known, but undocumented, area of the *tierra adentro*.

This journal, recorded daily by junior ecclesiastic Fray Francisco Silvestre Vélez de Escalante, followed the genre of like reports submitted to the king via governor and viceroy during the preceding two hundred fifty years of Spanish exploration and settlement in America. One need only read Hernando Cortés's *Letters to the Emperor* or Pedro de Cieza de León's *The Incas* to see the detail of the inventories taken wherever Spaniards traveled. Such reports are packed with information about what the observer experienced. Precious metals are reported where found, but more often the reports are concerned with areas suitable for settlement, potential for irrigated agriculture, dry farming, and pasturage. The *Domínguez-Escalante Journal* is no different.

Sections of the route documented in this journal were already known. At least one member of the party had traveled to the Gunnison River with an expedition led by Juan María de Rivera in 1765, eleven years earlier, and as far as the Colorado River in 1775. Recruits along the way provided valuable information about the region, introductions and translation services, and aided materially in satisfying logistical requirements for sometimes more than twenty humans, the horse herd, and the larder on the hoof.

The following introduction to the members of the party serves as a ready reference and shows, where possible, their duties performed.

Padre Fray Francisco Atanasio Domínguez, Commissary Visitor of the Custody of the Conversion of St. Paul, served as leader.

Padre Fray Francisco Silvestre Vélez de Escalante, minister and priest of Our Lady of Guadalupe, Zuni Pueblo, served as record keeper.

vii

Don Juan Pedro Cisneros, Chief Magistrate (*alcalde mayor*) of Zuni Pueblo.

Don Bernardo Miera y Pacheco, retired captain of militia and citizen of Santa Fe, was to map the route.

Don Joaquín Laín, citizen of Santa Fe.

Andrés Muñiz, interpreter and guide from Bernalillo. Muñiz spoke the Ute language and had served with the Juan María de Rivera expedition to the Gunnison River in 1765, and again traveled the region in 1775 with Pedro Mora and Gregorio Sandoval.

Lucrecio Muñiz, brother of Andrés Muñiz. A resident of Embudo, Lucrecio may well have accompanied his brother on a previous trip into the region.

Lorenzo Olivares, citizen of El Paso.

Juan de Aguilar, from Santa Clara.

Simón Lucero, from Zuni, was the servant of Don Juan Pedro Cisneros.

Felipe, a *coyote* (Spanish–Pueblo Indian mestizo) from Abiquiu who joined the expedition on 14 August 1776 near present-day Cahone, Colorado.

Juan Domingo, a *genízaro* (Hispanized plains Indian) from Abiquiu who joined the expedition with Felipe.

Atanasio, a Ute who joined on 24 August 1776 for payment of two large knives and sixteen strings of white glass beads. Atanasio received this name upon joining.

Francisco, a Laguna Ute initially named Silvestre, joined 30 August 1776. Six additional guides from the same Indian group accompanied the expedition for a time.

Joaquín, a Laguna Ute boy, became a member of the party on 2 September 1776.

This journal is a barometer of changing moods. There is the wonder of the bearded Indians, the first snowfall on 5 October, and three days later the realization that they are still a long way from Monterey. There is despair as food supplies dwindle to the point where pack horses, no longer needed for this role, are consumed. Fray Silvestre shares the late eighteenth-century Franciscan aim of Christianization and views indigenous cultures from the perspective of their potential for proselytization. Fray Silvestre also reminds us that the purpose of the expedition was to inventory the lands traversed and to document a route to California. He makes frequent comment concerning previous observers, complaining that "those who had come by here before had not informed us of this declivity," when describing the descent into the Grand Canyon near Castle Rock (Arizona). The tensions between Indian groups resurface in mid-November when Tano (formerly from Galisteo) residents of the Hopi pueblos argue for Spanish guards to be assigned to the Hopi to counter what was perceived as a threat from the Navajo. And there are the ever-present communication difficulties where the services of two and sometimes three interpreters are needed in an encounter.

The Domínguez-Escalante Journal is as timely today as it was in 1776 and in 1976. While the report contributes to belated interest in the Old Spanish Trail, a commercial and communication corridor connecting Santa Fe and Los Angeles as early as the start of the nineteenth century, its greatest value is that it provides a benchmark for comparison in the study of the Mountain West. Fray Silvestre's journal describes in detail the indigenous populations, plants, animals, watercourses, terrain, and potential of the route traversed, seen through eighteenth-century Spanish eyes. Dare we ask if human stewardship over the intervening centuries has improved upon the image reported in 1776?

—*Robert Himmerich y Valencia*
Peña Blanca, New Mexico

✠

INTRODUCTION

The Domínguez-Escalante journal of the 1776 expedition into the interior basin of Western America has been previously translated into English and published three times. A reasonable question is whether yet another version is necessary. We believe that it is.

The first English translation was published in 1909 by the Reverend W. R. Harris. Although it is a good pioneer effort, Harris relied entirely upon a typescript prepared for him from the imperfect 1854 version published in Spanish in Mexico City in *Documentos para la historia de Mexico*, segunda serie. Because of its numerous errors, both in translation and notes, it has been judged practically worthless by scholars. In 1945 Herbert S. Auerbach's *Father Escalante's Journal, 1776-77* appeared. He too relied primarily upon the 1854 version in *Documentos*, spot-checking various passages here and there with the Ayer manuscript in the Newberry Library, Chicago, Illinois. It is far superior to the Harris work, and Auerbach's notes and maps are especially useful, but it still contains mistakes because of the faulty source upon which he primarily relied. Herbert E. Bolton's *Pageant in the Wilderness* was the third English version to appear. The translation was apparently prepared by one of his graduate students, Miss Jessie Hazel Power, as a part of her M. A. program. She also relied mainly on the published Mexico City work, but checked some passages with manuscript copies from the Archivo General de Nación in Mexico City. These are later copies and also contain errors made by the scribes as they copied them. Bolton's long "Historical Introduction," while very well done, is virtually a paraphrasing of the journal with only an occasional editorial comment. His notes which accompany the text of the journal contain numerous errors.

It was therefore felt that, as a way to commemorate the two hundredth anniversary of the expedition during the bicentennial year of the United States, a new and definitive translation was appropriate in order to correct the numerous errors and false assumptions which have developed concerning it over the last half century and more.

This translation by Fray Angelico Chavez, a native New Mexico historian, poet, novelist, and Franciscan, is based primarily upon the earliest known manuscript copy of the journal. He has rendered it into readable, clear, and precise English and perhaps comes closest to the feelings and attitudes of the writers than heretofore.

The story of the Domínguez-Escalante expedition of 1776 is too well known to bear repeating in detail here. The general objective of opening an overland trail from Santa Fe, New Mexico, to the newly founded missions of California has been discussed many times. For a general summary of it the reader is referred to Bolton's discussion, mentioned above. It is expected that this translation and the notes which accompany it will enable the reader to follow precisely the expedition and to understand where the party traveled in relation to present-day geography and place-names. One should also gain an appreciation of the manifold day-to-day problems experienced by the travelers and a respect and admiration for the means they used in overcoming them as they blazed a new trail for over a thousand miles in unexplored and uncharted wilderness.

I should like now to attempt to dispel a number of misconceptions concerning the expedition. In the first place it was not the "Escalante Expedition," as it is so widely, yet erroneously, known. Auerbach called his work *Escalante's Journal* and considered it as his expedition. Bolton's subtitle to *Pageant in the Wilderness* is *The Story of the Escalante Expedition to the Interior Basin, 1776.* But it was not Escalante's expedition or journal alone. The actual leader of the enterprise and the man who had the major responsibility for undertaking, organizing, and directing it was Fray Francisco Atanasio Domínguez, Escalante's ecclesiastical superior in New Mexico and the one who, in fact, ordered Father Escalante to accompany him on the trip. It is not my purpose to downgrade or in any way detract from the contributions of Father Escalante, which were substantial, but to accord to Father Domínguez a measure of much-belated credit for the heavy burden of responsibility he bore in relation to the expedition, but for which he has rarely been recognized. It was he who had the task of making the difficult decisions while on the trail, disciplining the members of the party, and bearing the responsibility for the safety of the men and the ultimate success or failure of the expedition. Although the two Franciscans worked together as partners, a careful reading of the journal reveals that Father Domínguez was the actual leader. Father Escalante always recognized himself as the junior partner, but most historians who have concerned themselves with it have not. As Eleanor B. Adams has recently written:

*As the subordinate it was his [Escalante's] task to act as amanu-
ensis, but Domínguez was the man in charge and the one ulti-
mately accountable to their superiors; in view of his character, it
is incredible that he [Domínguez] should have delegated the entire responsibility to his younger colleague. The account reads
"we" throughout and both fathers signed it. In later years Vélez
de Escalante never referred to it except as "our diary," the one he
and Domínguez had kept during their journey. Fray Francisco
Atanasio was an equally keen, articulate, and interested observer,
and there can be no doubt that the report was a true collabora-
tion.*[1]

How is it, then, that Auerbach, Bolton, and others have made this
inversion and credited Father Escalante with the journal and the command of the expedition rather than Father Domínguez? One explana-
tion is that Vélez de Escalante had already established himself in the
minds of the authorities, both secular and ecclesiastical, as a remark-
ably able observer. His letters and reports on frontier conditions were
eagerly anticipated by higher authority. The authorities were already
familiar with Vélez de Escalante and his work. For his part, Father
Domínguez was virtually an unknown and because of the complaints
lodged against him by some of the New Mexico missionaries his repu-
tation was somewhat suspect. His report of the missions, his letters,
and his reports were almost totally ignored by his superiors. Whenever
the expedition was considered, it was Vélez de Escalante whose name
was recognized, and in this way perhaps it came to be regarded as his
expedition.

In fairness to both men, however, the expedition should be referred to as the "Domínguez-Escalante expedition," and the journal as
the "Domínguez-Escalante journal." For the past three years the
Domínguez-Escalante State-Federal Bicentennial Committee have
been directing their efforts toward this end and have insisted that this
designation be used whenever any reference is made to the event. It is
hoped that all those who have anything to do with teaching about or
discussing the expedition and journal in the future will accept and use
this proper designation and thereby help rectify a historical error
which has been perpetuated much too long.

1. Eleanor B. Adams, "Fray Francisco Atanasio Domínguez and Fray Silvestre
Vélez de Escalante," *Utah Historical Quarterly* 44 (Winter 1976): 53.

Another point which needs comment and clarification concerns the name of Fray Silvestre Vélez de Escalante. His contemporaries referred to him as "Fray Silvestre Vélez," or as "Fray Silvestre Vélez de Escalante," or as "Padre Vélez," or "Padre Vélez de Escalante." His surname was "Vélez," and therefore, to be absolutely correct in the matter, we should refer to him as such. Strictly speaking, then, the expedition should be known as the "Domínguez-Vélez Expedition." But since no one would know of whom or what we were speaking, we will have to perpetuate this error consciously and accept the name by which he has been known, Father Escalante, which name is but the birthplace of his father, Señor Vélez of the town of Escalante, Spain. Fray Silvestre Vélez de Escalante thus joins other Spanish pioneers whose family names have been virtually forgotten. For example, Coronado's name was Francisco Vásquez de Coronado, with Vásquez as the surname.[2] Also García López de Cárdenas, the discoverer of the Grand Canyon, and for a time credited with the European discovery of Utah, bore the family name of López. How did it happen that Fray Silvestre Vélez de Escalante came to be known simply as Escalante? It stems probably from the fact that Anglo writers, unfamiliar with the Spanish patronym and the manner in which Spaniards put their names together, simply assumed that the last name written was the family name and thus referred to him by this.

Incidentally, the name Escalante has also been perpetuated by numerous place-names, none of which were affixed by the explorers themselves (if they had done so we may have had a "Vélez" or two) or are even found, for the most part, along the route of march. Today Utah has an Escalante Desert, an Escalante River, an Escalante Forest, Escalante Mountains, an Escalante State Park, and a town of Escalante (there may be others). We would like, however, in this work, to give belated recognition to his true family name of Vélez. That [Vélez de] Escalante has had these numerous places named after him is still further evidence of the superior position ascribed to him—although, as we have seen, unfairly.

Until very recently—that is, until the efforts of the Domínguez-Escalante State-Federal Bicentennial Committee—there were no place-names in Utah to commemorate "the forgotten friar," Father

2. Neither Vásquez de Coronado nor López de Cárdenas held the title "don." During the first half of the sixteenth century, there were few noblemen with this title in New Spain. There is no doubt that Vásquez was a hidalgo and López had some claim to this status.

Domínguez. Steps are now being taken to name a "Domínguez Hill" at the mouth of Spanish Fork Canyon, from which the explorers first viewed the valley of Nuestra Señora de la Merced de los Timpanogotzis, or Utah Valley, as it is known today. The name "Domínguez Dome" has been suggested for the place where Father Domínguez preached a sermon and exhorted the men on October 11 to submit themselves wholly to the will of God and where they cast lots to determine whether to abandon the quest for Monterey or to press on. In a low spot in the east rim of Paria Canyon, near the Crossing of the Fathers, there is also a "Domínguez Pass," named in honor of Domínguez. Thus, some two hundred years after the expedition, Father Francisco Atanasio Domínguez is being remembered with place-names which are significant in that they are directly associated with important events along the trail itself.

As far as the results of the expedition are concerned, it was a failure. They did not reach their stated objective of Monterey and thereby open the overland route which they believed would be important for diplomatic, defensive, political, economic, and missionary purposes. But a historical event is sometimes more important for what failed to happen than for its actual immediate results. The Franciscans, so impressed with the Indians and the country in the Timpanogos (Utah) Valley, promised the natives that they would return within a year's time to teach them the gospel and bring tools and equipment, seeds, and cattle. It subsequently proved impossible for them to return, however. Conditions in New Mexico had deteriorated, and missionary efforts along the frontier declined. The Spanish government effected a retrenchment policy caused by the lack of money and men and aggravated by the expulsion of the Jesuits from the New World nine years earlier. The vacated Jesuit missions were to be manned by men of the other orders, and as there were not enough missionaries to occupy these it was impossible at the same time to extend the mission frontier to new and distant lands. Thus the hopes of Fathers Domínguez and Escalante to open a vast new mission field were dashed. Had the Franciscans been able to return to Utah, missions, pueblos, and a presidio would no doubt have been located there. Spanish customs, institutions, culture, and religion would have been firmly established and Utah would have become a settled and occupied part of the Spanish empire in the New World. Utah's history would have been closely entwined with that of New Mexico, California, and Texas. In the 1840s, when the Mormon leader Brigham Young sought a site for the future home of his exiled Saints, he may not have considered the Great Basin because it would have been already occupied and its best lands appropriated by Franciscan missions and Spanish settlers and soldiers. The failure of the Spaniards to capitalize on the information brought back by Fathers Domínguez and Escalante about central Utah was perhaps the most significant long-range result of the expedition. It meant, in effect, that Utah would not be permanently settled by white men for another seventy-one years and that it would then be by American Mormons rather than by Spanish Catholics. Dotting the Utah landscape would no doubt be communities with Spanish names such as Santa Catarina (Duchesne), Dulce Nombre de Jesús (Spanish Fork), San Antonio de Padua (Provo), San Nicolás (Springville), San Andrés (Payson), and Señor San José (Cedar City), instead of Mormon towns with names such as Lehi, Nephi, Manti, and Moroni.

A word should also be said about the subsequent careers of Fray Francisco Atanasio Domínguez and Fray Silvestre Vélez de Escalante following their "splendid wayfaring." Many writers have treated the two Franciscans as if they existed almost in a vacuum—that is, that they never did anything of note prior to the expedition and that once it was completed they returned to oblivion. Such is not the case. They were remarkable men who had interesting careers in New Mexico and Mexico both before and after the 1776 expedition.

Immediately upon his return from the Great Basin, Father Domínguez was recalled to Mexico to answer charges leveled at him by some of his disgruntled brethren in New Mexico—those whom he had found it necessary to discipline during his tour of inspection of the Franciscan missions there. He spent the remaining thirty years of his life in various missionary assignments on the northern frontiers of New Spain apparently trying, but in vain, to gain vindication for his conduct in New Mexico and recognition for a lifetime of selfless service to the Church. The report of his inspection of the missions was filed away in Mexico for 150 years and forgotten. Discovered in 1927, it was translated and published in 1956 and is a significant document which helps us understand conditions in New Mexico in that last quarter of the eighteenth century. This report establishes Fray Francisco Atanasio Domínguez as one of the most important Franciscans who ever labored in New Mexico, and his report is as significant for the eighteenth century as the Memorials of Fray Alonzo de Benavides were for the seventeenth.

Fray Silvestre Vélez de Escalante remained in New Mexico for several years after the expedition, serving as vice custos and as missionary at various Indian pueblos. In 1780 he requested permission to return to Mexico for treatment of the ailment which had given him such pain and discomfort during his labors in New Mexico. He died en route to Mexico City, in Parral, in April 1780. He was barely out of his twenties. Prior to departing from Santa Fe he concluded a survey of the Spanish archives there and wrote an epitome, or summary, of New Mexico history from 1693 to 1715, based upon documents, some of which are no longer extant. This history established Vélez de Escalante as an important historian of men, events, and affairs in late-seventeenth- and early-eighteenth-century New Mexico.

Thus Fathers Domínguez and Vélez de Escalante made important contributions in their own lifetimes as missionaries, teachers, scholars, historians, and explorers, and now, two hundred years down the stream of history, we remember *both* of them and commemorate their achievements with admiration and respect.

During the summer of 1975 a number of scholars conducted field research with the Chavez translation of the journal as a field guide. They carefully retraced the trail in a serious attempt to locate as precisely as possible the actual trail and the campsites of the 1776 expedition. Under the direction of Dr. David E. Miller, of the University of Utah, the following teams worked on different sections of the trail. From Santa Fe to the Colorado border (covering the expedition's travels of July 29 through August 5, 1776) were Dr. W. Alan Minge, Dr. Robert Archibald, and Mr. W. L. Rusho; in southwestern Colorado (from August 5 through August 26, 1776), Dr. Robert W. Delaney and Mr. Robert McDaniel; along the western portion of Colorado (August 27 through September 9, 1776), Dr. Floyd A. O'Neil and Mr. Gregory C. Thompson; also western Colorado and into Utah (September 8 through September 16, 1776), Mr. G. Clell Jacobs; from the point where the expedition entered the present state of Utah to the Utah Valley (September 13 through September 23, 1776), Msgr. Jerome Stoffel and Mr. George Stewart; from Utah Lake to the Arizona border (September 25 through October 15, 1776), Dr. Ted J. Warner, Dr. Thomas G. Alexander, Mr. Stewart Jacobson, and Mr. David E. Vickstrom; and from this point to Santa Fe (October 16 through January 2, 1777), Dr. C. Gregory Crampton, Mr. W. L. Rusho, and Dr. David E. Miller.

The field reports of each of these teams were utilized in the preparation of the notes which accompany this work. Appreciation and thanks are extended to each of these individuals. In the intervening two hundred years since the padres passed this way, the traces of much of the trail have been obliterated by the march of progress and the growth, development, and construction of towns, cities, highways, farms, dams, railroads, etc. However, so conscientiously did the field researchers approach their assignment that there can be little question that this is the most faithful and accurate delineation of the trail and the location of the campsites as is possible under the circumstances.

Appreciation and thanks are also extended to anyone who helped in any way to make this present work possible.

Ted J. Warner

✠

TRANSLATOR'S NOTE

There are at least nine manuscript copies extant, scattered throughout European and New World libraries, of the 1776 diary kept by Fray Silvestre Vélez de Escalante during that memorable trek he made through much of our great Southwest in the company of some Hispanic and mixed-breed laymen under the leadership of his close friend and religious superior, Fray Francisco Atanasio Domínguez. That he consulted daily on "our diary" with his compatible superior can be assumed from this very fact, as well as from the tenor or flavor of many a passage. For Domínguez himself was a very observant and at times witty or sarcastic writer, as we gather from a detailed report on the New Mexico missions which he had completed in the first half of that same year.

Since it also minutely described Pueblo Indian and Hispanic life, besides churches and missionaries, an annotated translation of this report, entitled *Missions of New Mexico, 1776* (Albuquerque, 1956), has been reprinted by the state of New Mexico as one of its historical contributions to our national Bicentennial.

When dispatched from Mexico City to New Mexico as commissary visitor of its missions, Domínguez had also been charged to discover a more or less direct route from Santa Fe to the recently established garrison and town of Monterey on the California coast, but not without an option to explore new mission possibilities en route. No sooner was the small expedition well on its way, however, than fervent missionaries Domínguez and Escalante began exercising this option so enthusiastically that the second half of 1776 was spent wandering and tarrying among the nomadic Indian tribes throughout what is the wide Four Corners area now comprising the states of Utah, Colorado, Arizona, and New Mexico. An approaching severe winter and many serious mishaps among the mazes of the Grand Canyon forced the party to abandon the trip to Monterey and return to Santa Fe by way of the Hopi pueblos at year's end. Nonetheless, the resulting diary, wonderfully describing every detail of rugged and scenic country along with the qualities and customs of its aborigines, and no less the participants' heroic adventures—as also the very year in which all this took place—have now furnished the four states concerned with an ideal historical contribution to our national Bicentennial by collaborating in the issuing of this new translation.

It was a rather late inspiration, and, for this very reason, lack of time prevented an assemblage of all the known manuscripts for a detailed comparison, the translating and editing of which could entail years of labor. Also out of the question was the addition of numberless annotations of historical, philological, ethnical, and other points of interest which almost every paragraph of the diary so richly suggests. The only manuscript copies readily at hand were at the Newberry Library (Ayer Collection) in Chicago, the Archivo General de la Nación (AGN, Mexico), and the Archivo General de Indias (AGI, Seville); but at the very start there occurred a windfall of sorts when I discovered that the Newberry copy was in the handwriting of Fray José Palacio, who had acted as secretary to Domínguez during the latter's visitation of the New Mexico missions earlier in 1776. Since this manuscript came from the Ramirez Mexican Collection, which consisted of much material rifled from Franciscan headquarters in Mexico City during one of many revolutions, the inference is that this was the very first copy made in Santa Fe from the original, and subsequently sent down to the Mother Province of the Holy Gospel in that very same year.

Furthermore, while this Newberry copy is far from neat and hence difficult to read, as if done hastily with no regard to careful penmanship, an attempt at accuracy was not neglected. Father Palacio, if not Escalante himself, took great pains going over it in order to make many small emendations. Here we can very well suppose that, sometime after the signed original was delivered to Governor Mendinueta on January 3, 1777, it was borrowed back for the time required for this copy to be hurriedly made in Santa Fe.

This Newberry manuscript has now been compared with the Seville, or AGI, which was most neatly done in Mexico City by some official scrivener and attested to by Antonio Bonilla, Mexico, July 26, 1777. This scribe skipped sentences or phrases here and there, evidently not checking back to make any corrections, while substituting better spelling or terms for certain archaisms or Latinisms peculiar to those early mission friars. There are also a couple or more phrases redounding to the glory of the Crown or to Spaniards in general which the Franciscan (Newberry) copy does not have.

The third comparison was made with the AGN copy, likewise a fine example of penmanship, done twenty years later in Chihuahua and attested to by a Manuel Merino, June 22, 1797. It is a much better one than the AGI in many respects, but the main value of both these secular manuscripts was in helping to clarify Father Palacio's script wherever some words were smudged or too pinched for clarity.

Needless to say, reference was also made to the two English translations by Auerbach and Bolton. The former, as its author himself stated, was based on a printed edition in *Documentos para la Historia de México* (Mexico, 1854), with only "random excerpts spot checked" with the Newberry manuscript. Hence, for one example, he missed a brief but important paragraph evidently absent in the printed version. Similarly, Professor Bolton, whose combined translation of the diary and priceless review of the entire journey in *Pageant in the Wilderness* (Utah State Historical Society, 1951, 1972) is still a most remarkable accomplishment, appears to have leaned on Auerbach's earlier translation—keeping the omission mentioned and other peculiarities, and with just about the same random spot-checking with the three manuscript copies detailed above. What is likewise common to both of these translations is that they were simply done by the dictionary, that is, with no heed to archaic or strictly local expressions and terminology.

While naturally having both Spanish and English dictionaries at my elbow, I mainly listened to Padre Escalante (and his companions) speaking as I read the text aloud to myself. This was not only as a Spaniard or a Mexican would, but also as a twelfth-generation Hispanic New Mexican with an ear for the language of the times and the locale would—and as one thoroughly conversant with ecclesiastical and Franciscan terminology along with the style in which those eighteenth-century friars expressed themselves. As for the style of English employed, it is the result of writing and publishing poetry and prose in the language for the past four decades.

However, this humble expertise ended here, for I did not have any personal knowledge, unfortunately, of the topography covered by the diary—something just as paramount for rendering geographical and related features more faithfully. Naturally, I ceded complete liberty to those individuals who have an intimate knowledge of the terrain, for them to ascertain whether, for example, Escalante's *arroyos* were mere washes or deep canyons, or his *álamos* cottonwoods or mountain poplars or aspens.

As some have suggested, a glossary on the flora and fauna, and particularly on strictly local extralexicon terminology, would have been in

order, had time allowed. Now, if only we had the original with the sig-
natures of Padres Domínguez and Escalante—if, in fact, it does exist
somewhere—most of this hasty labor, and this preface, could have
been nicely dispensed with.

Fray Angelico Chavez
Sante Fe, New Mexico

THE
DOMÍNGUEZ-ESCALANTE
JOURNAL

✠

SANTA FE–RÍO DE SAN LÁZARO
JULY 29–AUGUST 11

July 29, 1776

On July 29 of the year 1776, under the patronage of the Virgin Mary Our Lady conceived without original sin, and of the thrice-holy Joseph her most blessed spouse, we, Fray[1] Francisco Atanasio Domínguez,[2] current commissary visitor[3] of the Custody of the Conversion of St. Paul in New Mexico,[4] and Fray Francisco Silvestre Vélez de Escalante,[5]

1. A contraction of *fraile* ("friar"), used only as a title by the religious of certain orders, never as a substantive and never apart from the first, or religious, name. It may be used with the full name of a friar, but never with the surname alone.

2. Born in Mexico City about 1740, he joined the Franciscan order in 1757 at the age of seventeen. The first known reference to him is at the Convent of Veracruz as Commissary of the Third Order in October 1772, when he was thirty-two years old and in the order fifteen years. In 1775 he was sent to New Mexico from the Mexican Province of the Holy Gospel to make an inspection of the Custody of the Conversion of St. Paul. He arrived in Santa Fe on March 22, 1776. He was also under instructions to investigate the possibility of opening an overland route between Santa Fe and Monterey, California. In 1777 he was recalled to Mexico and served as chaplain of presidios in Nueva Vizcaya. He was at Janos, Sonora, Mexico, in 1800. He died sometime between 1803 and 1805. See Eleanor B. Adams and Fray Angelico Chavez, eds. and trans., *The Missions of New Mexico, 1776: A Description by Fray Francisco Atanasio Domínguez with Other Contemporary Documents* (Albuquerque: University of New Mexico Press, 1956), for additional biographical information.

3. A commissary visitor is one to whom a special task is committed. Used in this sense in Domínguez' title as Commissary Visitor, it empowered him to act for his provincial in a formal inspection of the New Mexican missions. This office was given only to clergymen of the highest caliber, and there can be no doubt that Father Domínguez at that time enjoyed esteem at headquarters for his learning and mature judgment.

4. When his followers became so numerous that they had to be divided into groups, St. Francis chose this term in preference to *abbey* or other more formal designations. After his time the large groups adopted the term *province*, using *custody* for smaller groups dependent on a full-fledged province. This was the status of the Custody of the Conversion of St. Paul in New Mexico, which was dependent on the Province of the Holy Gospel in Mexico City for more than two centuries (Adams and Chavez, *Missions*, pp. 354–55).

5. Born in the mountains of Santander in the town of Treceño, Spain, about 1750, he took the Franciscan habit in the Convento Grande in Mexico City when he was seventeen years old. He came to New Mexico in 1774 and was stationed first at Laguna

3

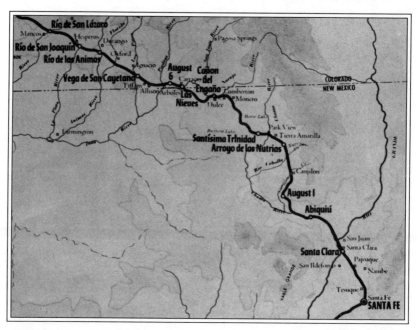

SANTA FE TO RÍO DE SAN LÁZARO, JULY 29–AUGUST 11

minister and priest of the mission of Nuestra Señora de Guadalupe de Zuni[6]—voluntarily accompanied by Don[7] Juan Pedro Cisneros,[8] chief

---

pueblo and then, in January 1775, was assigned to Zuni. He continued to be its minister until summoned by Domínguez to Santa Fe in June the following year. He remained in New Mexico for two years following his return from this expedition. He died in Parral, Mexico, in April 1780, while returning to Mexico City for medical treatment. He was scarcely thirty years old. See Adams and Chavez, *Missions*, for additional biographical data. See also Eleanor B. Adams, "Fray Silvestre and the Obstinate Hopi," *New Mexico Historical Review* 38 (1963): 97–138.

6. This church, begun in 1706, still stands in the center of the Zuni village. It was abandoned in 1821, and the buildings fell into ruins. By action of the Zuni tribe, the Catholic Diocese of Gallup, and the National Park Service, the church was completely restored in 1968. A Zuni artist is presently completing a series of murals inside the mission, depicting various Kachinas so important to their ancient religion. These paintings, juxtaposed with Catholic stations of the cross, demonstrate the ability of Indian concepts to survive.

7. Honorary title of great dignity which originally was given only to those of the top rank of nobility and which later was given to all the nobility. In the eighteenth century, as well as today, it is applied to any distinguished person. It is a title of respect used with the first, or Christian, name or with the full name, but never with the surname alone.

8. Nothing is known about him other than the references to him in this journal.

magistrate of the said Pueblo de Zuni; Don Bernardo Miera y Pacheco,[9] retired captain of militia and citizen of La Villa de Santa Fe; Don Joaquín Laín,[10] citizen of the same Villa; Lorenzo Olivares[11] from La Villa de Paso; Andrés Muñiz,[12] Lucrecio Muñiz, [13] Juan de Aguilar,[14] and Simón Lucero[15]—after the aforementioned had implored the protection of our thrice-holy patron saints and received the Holy Eucharist, set out from La Villa de Santa Fe, capital of this kingdom of New Mexico, and at the end of nine leagues arrived at El Pueblo de Santa Clara,[16] where we spent the night. Today nine leagues[17] to the northwest.

9. Native of Valle De Carriedo, Montañas de Burgos. Came with his family from Chihuahua to El Paso in 1743, thence to Santa Fe in 1754–56. He was an army engineer, merchant, Indian fighter, government agent, rancher, artist, and cartographer. It was believed at one time that Father Vélez de Escalante had recommended that he lead the expedition bound for Monterey; however, Escalante denied this and stated that he should not command the expedition but make a map of the terrain explored. And it was "only for this do I consider him useful." In 1778 he prepared an interesting and useful map of the country traversed by the expedition. Miera y Pacheco was a painter and sculptor, and his works appeared in many New Mexico mission churches. His large painting of St. Michael still stands on the altar screen in Santa Fe's chapel of San Miguel. Some of his statuettes were in the Zuni church. Father Domínguez was harshly critical of Miera's artwork. Miera also prepared a report on the expedition which is included in Herbert E. Bolton, *Pageant in the Wilderness: The Story of the Escalante Expedition to the Interior Basin, 1776* (Salt Lake City: Utah State Historical Society, 1951), pp. 243–50.

10. Native of Santa Cruz, near Coca, in Castilla la Vieja. He died in 1799.

11. No additional data have come to light concerning him.

12. From Bernalillo, New Mexico. Knew the Ute language and served as interpreter. He had been with Juan María de Rivera to the Gunnison River in 1775.

13. Brother of Andrés Muñiz, another member of the expedition. From Embudo, north of Santa Fe.

14. Born in Santa Clara, New Mexico. No other data available.

15. Perhaps from Zuni. He was servant to Don Pedro Cisneros.

16. This Tewa pueblo, which was named Santa Clara by Don Juan de Oñate in 1598, is situated on the west bank of the Rio Grande, 20 miles northwest of Santa Fe and 1 1/2 miles south of Espanola, New Mexico.

17. A Spanish league in the eighteenth century was the equivalent of 2.63 U.S. statute miles today. Eighteenth-century travelers calculated a league as the distance traveled for one hour on horseback over level terrain at a normal gait. Thus, on this date, the expedition journeyed nine leagues and therefore covered some 23.67 miles. They were in the saddle for at least nine hours. Reckoning distance in this manner is obviously a haphazard method at best, and accounts for the fact that in retracing the route it is difficult to understand the long distances traveled on certain days. It has been claimed that a man on horseback in level country could travel as much as 20–30 leagues a day, or 52–66 miles!

July 30

On the 30th we traveled another nine leagues, more or less, and arrived at El Pueblo de Santa Rosa de Abiquiú,[18] where, due to various circumstances, we stayed over through the 31st without undertaking a day's march; and by means of a solemn high mass we once more implored the aid of our thrice-holy patron saints.

August 1

On the 1st of August, after both of us had celebrated the holy sacrifice of the mass, we set out westward from El Pueblo de Santa Rosa de Abiquiú along the box channel of El Río de Chama[19] and, after having gone through it a little less than a league, swung to the northwest; then, after about three and a half leagues of bad going because there are some little mesas very much strewn with rocks, we paused to rest on the north side of El Valle de la Piedra Alumbre,[20] close to the dry arroyo. They say that there is rock alum and transparent gypsum in some mesas which stand to the east and northeast of this valley. By afternoon we set out northward from the dry arroyo, took to the northeast a short distance away through a wooded canyon, and after two leagues of very bad going halted at the edge of said arroyo. Today a good heavy downpour caught us, and we traveled seven leagues.[21]

18. Should be called Santo Tomás de Abiquiú. Santa Rosa de Abiquiú is the ancestor of the modern Hispanic village of Abiquiu, which overlooks the Chama River from its perch high upon the left bank. Abiquiu is a pleasant town, retaining many of the characteristics of an earlier age. Residents have an exhilarating view of the Chama Valley to the jagged sandstone cliffs beyond. Abiquiu was on the frontier and was the last contact which the explorers had with a Spanish settlement for the duration of the journey, and one can readily imagine the final rush to complete provisions and send final messages, and the anticipation with which the group prepared to move on. The trail from Santa Fe to Abiquiu was well known and well traveled, since it was within the Hispanicized area of New Mexico. The explorers remained here for two nights. In 1830 Abiquiu became the "Gateway to the Old Spanish Trail." For information on early Spanish settlement in the Chama Valley, see Frances Leon Swadesh, *Los Primeros Pobladores: Hispanic Americans of the Ute Frontier* (Notre Dame: University of Notre Dame Press, 1974).
19. Tributary of the Rio Grande. Its source is El Vado Lake. The Spaniards had occupied the Chama River Valley for a hundred years when the expedition passed through it.
20. Today New Mexicans render this as one word: *Piedralumbre*.
21. About 18.5 miles.

August 2

On the 2nd of August we continued northeast along the same canyon, and at a little more than a quarter league we swung north. We entered through a wooded canyon in which for a quarter league's distance there is a scruboak thicket so dense that in it four horses vanished from our sight while passing through, so that we had to make a halt in order to look for them. They were found within a short time. And though we lost the path in this thicket for its being little used, we later saw that it went along the east side of the arroyo which runs through its middle; it is the same one which farther down we call Arroyo del Canjilón,[22] a dry arroyo. Past the thicket there is a short plain of abundant pasturage and one very pleasant to see, because it produces certain rosettes having a tint between purple and white which, if they are not carnations, are very much like those of the same color.

There are also clumps of *lemita*,[23] which is a red bead the size of the blackthorn's, and its coolness and taste very similar to the lemon's, so that in this country it is regarded as its substitute for making cool drinks. Besides this there is chokecherry, very much smaller than the one of the valley of Mexico, and another tiny fruit here called *manzanita*[24] the bush of which is like the *lemita's* but the leaf more like that of celery. The little fruit's size is almost that of ordinary chickpeas, the color white in some and black in others, the taste a sharp bittersweet but agreeable.

Where the rosettes mentioned begin, the canyon is split in two by a tall mesa which enters it in this wise. There are trails through both of them, one of which goes north and the other west. Where the latter begins, and below the southern point of said mesa, there is a small spring of good perennial flow; however, for the horse herds to drink even a little of it, it will be necessary to dig waterholes. When the horses turned up we continued our day's march westward along the canyon and trail, having traveled a league and a quarter to the north. After going less than half a league to the west, we swung northwest, and after a little more than three leagues' travel over good terrain we

22. Still called the *Canjilon* today.
23. Squawbush. See Rubén Cobos, *A Dictionary of New Mexico and Southern Colorado Spanish* (Santa Fe: Museum of New Mexico Press, 1983).
24. Still called a *manzanita*. There is no English equivalent for it.

arrived to take a rest at an arroyo which is called El Río de la Cebolla,[25] getting away from the trail a bit. In its sunken bed we found plenty of still water, for it seldom flows with it, according to indications.

From here we set out in the afternoon, going up northward for about a quarter league to take up the trail we had left. We turned to the northwest, and after a little more than three leagues of good terrain we stopped on a short plain and at the edge of another arroyo which is called El Río de las Nutrias;[26] for although it does not have water running permanently it apparently keeps it throughout all or most of the year in banked ponds where beaver are said to breed. Today eight leagues.[27]

August 3

On the 3rd we set out, headed northwest from El Arroyo de las Nutrias, entered a small pine forest, and, after traveling a little less than three leagues, descended to El Río de Chama and went up north for about a mile[28] over its pretty meadow. We forded it and stopped to rest on the opposite side. The river ford is good, but on the margins nearby there are big hidden sinkholes covered over with thin rubble. In one of them Don Juan Pedro Cisneros' mount got completely submerged. The river's meadow is about a league long from north to south, good land for farming with the help of irrigation; it produces a great deal of good flax and abundant pasturage. There are also the other prospects which a settlement requires for its founding and maintenance. Here it has a good grove of white poplar.

In the afternoon we went on and, after climbing the river's west slope, came into a small valley which we named Santa Domingo.[29] It is surrounded by three large pine-forested mesas which, starting with three small mounts that they have somewhat to the north, form a half arc from north to south until they reach the river. They told us that to the west of these mesas there were two lakes, the first and southernmost to the west of the gap which from the slope mentioned is seen

25. Means "Onion River." It is still called the Cebolla today.
26. Means "Beaver River." It is still referred to as the Nutrias River.
27. About 21 miles.
28. A Spanish mile equals 2.634 English miles. It was thus just slightly more than a Spanish league.
29. This valley is formed by Willow Creek, which has now been dammed to form Heron Lake.

between the first and second mesas, and the second to the west of the next gap which also can be seen between the second and third mesas. These lakes with the valley mentioned are very suitable for raising large and small livestock.

We continued northwest through the valley and entered a small pine forest; in it a loaded mule strayed off and did not turn up until after sundown, so that we had to halt on broken brambly ground next to the three small mounts mentioned, which we named La Santísima Trinidad,[30] after having traveled only two leagues northwest from the river. There is no water at this site, although we found a little in an arroyo to the east-southeast near the broken ground. Where we crossed it today, El Río de Chama runs from north to south; from a little before it fronts El Cerro del Pedernal[31] west to east until it passes El Pueblo de Abiquiú. Today five leagues.[32]

August 4

On the 4th we set out northward from El Paraje de la Santísima Trinidad. We went two leagues through the same forest, which consists of pines, some piñons, and scruboaks. It also abounds in pasturage and very tall-growing flax. It is fenced about by two large mesas, both of which by forming a semicircle almost come together at their points, the first's northerly and the second's southerly one—a small narrow gap or pass separating them. We marched northwest about a quarter league and passed through the little gap where another lake begins, which we named Olivares,[33] and which must be a quarter league in length and in

30. "The Most Holy Trinity." Located about five miles southwest of Park View.
     Note: *Throughout these notes many sites are located with reference to modern towns, buildings, business establishments, etc., which did not exist at the time of the expedition. For brevity, and to avoid excessive repetition, such phrases as "near the site of present-day . . . " and "two miles south of where . . . now stands" are often given simply as "near . . . ," and "two miles south of. . . ." Thus, by "five miles southwest of Park View" the reader should understand "five miles southwest of the location of the modern town of Park View."*
31. "Flint Hill." Located a few miles southwest of Abiquiu. It was known to the Tewa Indians in the area as the flaking stone, flint, or obsidian mountain. Ancient mine workings here produced native chert or flinty material which was used in fashioning weapons and craft tools.
32. Thirteen miles.
33. Named after Lorenzo Olivares of El Paso, a member of the expedition. It is now called Horse Lake. It is located in a secluded valley of the Jicarilla Apache Indian Reservation.

width two hundred yards, more or less. Its waters, even if not very pal-
atable, are fit to drink.

From the lake and small gap we proceeded north for half a league
and swung to the northwest, leaving the trail which goes toward La
Piedra Parada[34] (a site known to our people who have traveled through
here), and the guides directed us through a sagebrush stretch without
path or trail whatsoever, saying that there were three very troublesome
inclines on the trail we were leaving, and that it was less direct than the
straight way we were taking.

We went a little more than a league, and on the same sagebrush
stretch turned to the west-northwest; we again entered the forest
(which continues), and at half a league we took to the northwest. We
traveled three leagues and a half through a narrow valley most richly
abounding with pastures and arrived at a very spacious meadow of the
arroyo which along the said trail of La Piedra Parada they call El Belduque.[35] On the meadow we swung to the west, and after going two
leagues down the arroyo we halted in a canyon which, on account of a
certain incident, we named El Cañón del Engaño.[36] Today nine leagues
and a quarter.[37] There is plenty of ponded water here, and pasturage.

August 5

On the 5th we left El Cañón del Engaño toward the southwest, and at
half a league we reached El Río de Navajo,[38] which rises in La Sierra de
la Grulla;[39] it runs from northeast to southwest up to here, whence it
turns north a little more than three leagues until it joins another river
which they call San Juan.[40] Here the said Navajo carried less water than
the Chama. Having crossed the river, we continued with difficulty

34. This is Chimney Rock, a conspicuous landmark close to U.S. Highway 160.
35. A *belduque* was a long hunting knife and a standard item of trade with nomadic Indians. Just why they called this trail by this name is unknown. Perhaps they
gave an Indian such a knife at this point. It is identified as Amargo Creek today.
36. "Canyon of Deceit." They do not elaborate on what the incident was which
caused them to name it this. It is located on Amargo Creek about 1.3 miles above its
junction with the Navajo River.
37. About 24 miles.
38. The Navajo River today.
39. "The Crane Mountains." Perhaps they saw birds they identified as cranes
here. Today these are the Rocky Mountains. The San Juan River watershed includes the
southerly drainage from Wolf Creek Pass, which connects the San Juan Basin with the
San Luis Valley to the east.
40. Still called the San Juan River. It discharges into the Colorado River.

through the same canyon for nearly a league to the south. We swung southwest a quarter league and three-quarters west through canyons, over inclines, and through very troublesome tree growth. The experts lost the trail—and even the slight acquaintance they showed to have had with this terrain. And so, to avoid going farther down, we took to the northwest. We traveled without trail for about three leagues, going up a high mount but without a steep grade, and we caught sight of the said arroyo's sunken channel. We went over to it down slopes which were rather rough yet negotiable, and at a little more than three leagues west-northwest we crossed it at a good ford and halted on the northern side. Here it is already joined with that of the San Juan.

The experts said that these two rivers came together a little farther up, and so we decided to take the latitude of this stopping-point and held up for this purpose until the afternoon of the following day. A bearing was taken by the sun's meridian and we found the place, which we named Nuestra Señora de las Nieves,[41] to be at 37° 51′ latitude.[42] Fray Silvestre went out to inspect the place where the said rivers of Navajo and San Juan come together, and found that it lay three leagues as the crow flies almost due east of Las Nieves, and that on either one's banks at the junction itself there were good prospects for a moderate settlement.

El Río de San Juan carries more water than the Navajo, and they say that farther north it has good and large meadows because it flows over more open country. Together they now form a river as plenteous as El Norte in the month of July, and it is called Río Grande de Navajo for separating the province of this name from the Yuta nation. Starting down from the meadow and Paraje de Nuestra Señora de las Nieves, there is good land with prospects for irrigation and everything needed for three or four settlements, even if they be large ones[43]—that is, from

41. "Our Lady of the Snows." The site was so named because of the vista of snow-covered peaks from the campsite, which was located at Carracas, Colorado, on the north bank of the San Juan River in the vicinity of a bridge about 1/8 mile off the gravel road that goes to Pagosa Junction and on to Pagosa Springs, but they would have seen them from the high ground before descending to the San Juan River. Carracas is a deserted station on the abandoned Denver and Rio Grande Railroad line.

42. Their calculations were somewhat too high. Carracas, Colorado, is located at 37° 1′ 30″. Pagosa Springs is 37° 16′.

43. It is interesting to note how the padres suggested sites for future Spanish settlements along the route of the march. They did this throughout the expedition,

what we saw. On either edge of the river there are leafy and extremely dense thickets of white poplar, scruboak, chokecherry, *manzanita*, *lemita*, and gooseberry. There is also some sarsaparilla and a tree that looks to us like the walnut. Today eight leagues.[44]

August 6

On the 6th in the afternoon we set out from El Paraje de Nuestra Señora de las Nieves, downstream and to the west, and after traveling two and a half leagues of bad terrain we halted by the river's edge. Don Bernardo Miera had been having stomach trouble all along and this afternoon he got much worse, but God willed that he got better before morning the next day so that we could continue on our way. Today two leagues and a half.[45]

August 7

On the 7th we continued west along the river's edge and adjacent mesas' slopes for a little more than a league, and we went up a difficult incline. We turned northwest, and after another league we arrived at the river called La Piedra Parada, very near to where it joins the Navajo. Here it has a very large meadow, which we named San Antonio,[46] of very good land for farming with the help of irrigation, together with all the rest that a settlement requires by way of firewood, stone, timber, and pastures—and all close by. This river rises to the north of the San Juan in the same Sierra de la Grulla, runs from north to south, and is a little smaller than the Chama where it passes through El Pueblo de Abiquiú. Having crossed this river we traveled west two leagues, somewhat more than another two west-northwest, and arrived at the western edge of the river called Los Pinos because some grow along its edges. It consists of very good water and is a bit smaller than El Norte;[47] it flows through here from north to south, enters the Navajo, and rises out of La Sierra de la Grulla near its western end, where they call it Sierra de la Plata.[48] Here it has a large meadow, very abundant with

---

picking out the best sites which they one day expected would be thriving Spanish communities.

44. Slightly over 21 miles by their calculations.

45. About 6.5 miles.

46. Name not applied to this place today. It was the flat land close to the San Juan River west of Carracas, Colorado. It is in irrigated crops now.

47. They were doubtless referring to the Rio Grande.

48. Means "The Silver Mountains." The La Plata Mountains today.

pastures, especially of grama grass, extensive and good lands for farming through irrigation, with all the rest that may be desired for a goodly
settlement. We stopped in it, naming it La Vega de San Cayetano.[49] Today a little more than six leagues.[50]

August 8

On the 8th we set out west-northwest from La Vega de San Cayetano
and Río de los Pinos,[51] and at the end of four leagues arrived at El Río
Florido,[52] which is medium sized and smaller than that of Los Pinos. It
rises in the same sierra farther to the west, and where we crossed it has
a larger meadow, of good land for farming with the aid of irrigation.
The pastures on the meadow are good, but not in the immediate vicinity, although it evidently has them in wet years. Having crossed El
Río Florido, we traveled west two leagues and west-northwest a little
more than another two. We went down a rocky and not too lengthy
incline and arrived at El Río de las Ánimas,[53] near the western point of
La Sierra de la Plata where it has its origin. We crossed it and halted on
the opposite side. It is as large as El Norte, and now carried somewhat
more water and with greater rapidity, because here its currents, which
run from north to south, have a steeper fall, and it flows like the foregoing ones into the Navajo. Through here it runs through a box channel, but farther down it is said to have good meadows. Today eight
leagues, a little more.[54] There is no good pasturage here, but there is
some a little farther on.

August 9

On the 9th we set out from El Río de las Ánimas and ascended the
incline west of the river, which, although it is not too lengthy, is quite
difficult, consisting of plenty of rock and being very steep in places. We

49. The flat land along the Pine River south of Ignacio, Colorado. The name is
not in use today in that area.
50. Close to 16 miles.
51. The Río de los Pinos is the Pine River and is still so designated on some maps.
52. The Florida River. They crossed it in the vicinity of the present bridge on
Colorado State Highway 172. Downstream from here the land is quite rocky and arid,
although near the bridge there is good pasturage, alluded to in the diary.
53. Probably somewhat south of Colorado State Highway 172 toward Farmington
Hill, which they descended to the Animas River and crossed it. They camped on the
Animas River, on its west bank, on a level spot directly west of the livestock sale barn
about four miles south of the city limits of Durango, Colorado.
54. Twenty-one miles.

passed the small forest on its crest,[55] with which it must measure a little more than a quarter of a league. We entered a narrow valley of abundant pastures,[56] traveled through it one league to the west, and turned west by northwest; then, after going three leagues through a leafy forest of good pasturage, we reached El Río de San Joaquín—de la Plata[57] by another name—which is small and similar to the one which passes through El Pueblo de San Geronimo of the Taos Indians.[58]

It rises at the same western point of La Sierra de la Plata and descends through the same canyon in which there are said to be veins and outcroppings of metallic ore. However, although years ago certain individuals from New Mexico came to inspect them by order of the governor, who at the time was Don Tomás Vález Cachupín, and carried back metal-bearing rocks, it was not ascertained for sure what kind of metal they consisted of. The opinion which some formed previously, from the accounts of various Indians and from some citizens of the kingdom, that they were silver ore, furnished the sierra with this name.

From the aforesaid incline by El Río de las Ánimas to this Río de San Juan, the terrain is very moist, since it rains very frequently because of its proximity to the sierra; as a result, both in the mountain forest—which consists of very tall and straight pines, scruboak, and several kinds of wild fruits—and in its narrow valleys there are the prettiest of pastures. The climate here is excessively cold even in the months of July and August. Among the fruits mentioned there grows a small one of black hue, pleasant taste, and looking very much like the medlar[59] if not that sweet. We did not proceed ahead today because the mounts had not fed enough the night before and were rather weak by now, and also because a thick and prolonged heavy downpour made us halt.[60] Today four leagues and a quarter,[61] almost all to the west.

55. This small forest has long since been cut down, but at that time it probably contained large ponderosa pines.
56. Ridges Basin.
57. Called simply La Plata today.
58. The stream mentioned is the Taos Creek, which flows through the Pueblo of Taos, New Mexico, and divides the village in two.
59. Similar to a crabapple.
60. The campsite was on the La Plata River at the site of Hesperus, from which they could see the hill they had to skirt to get to the Mancos drainage.
61. Eleven miles.

August 10

On the 10th—although Padre Fray Francisco Atanasio awoke in bad condition because of a rheumy flow[62] in his face and head which he had begun experiencing the day before, and it was necessary to tarry awhile until he could breathe better—the steady rains, the weather's inclemency, and the great humidity of the place forced us to leave it by heading north; after going a little more than a league we turned northwest. We traveled one league and turned west through very pleasant narrow valleys with woods, very abundant with pastures, with different blooms and flowers, and after about two leagues a very thick downpour caught us again. Padre Fray Francisco Atanasio got worse, the trail became impossible, and so, after very painfully traveling another two leagues to the west, we found ourselves obliged to halt at the edge of the first rivulet of the two which make up the San Lázaro[63]—of the Mancos by another name. The pasturages continued in great abundance. Today four leagues and half.[64]

August 11

On the 11th, notwithstanding the severe cold and wetness we were now experiencing, we were unable to change our location, for Padre Fray Francisco Atanasio awoke very much exhausted from the trouble mentioned, and with some fever. For this reason we could not go over to see the sierra's metallic veins and rocks mentioned,[65] even though they were a short distance away, as one companion who had seen them on another occasion assured us.[66]

62. Father Domínguez had caught a bad head cold with its attendant runny nose.

63. The Mancos River. Campsite was on the East Mancos River just before its confluence with the main Mancos River.

64. About 11.8 miles.

65. These "veins and rocks" in the La Plata Mountains had been mentioned by earlier expeditions into the area.

66. Refers to Andrés Muñiz, who had been with the Juan María de Rivera expedition of 1765 and perhaps on later expeditions as well.

✠

RÍO DE SAN LÁZARO—
SAN RAMÓN
AUGUST 12–AUGUST 31

August 12

On the 12th Padre Fray Francisco Atanasio awoke somewhat improved, and more to change terrain and weather than to gain a day's march, we set out from the site and Río de San Lázaro toward the northwest. We traveled [*crossed out:* a little more than a league, turned west by west-northwest] five leagues through leafy tree-growth with good pasturage, took to the west, went two leagues and a half through a sagebrush stretch of little pasturage, and, after a quarter league of travel toward the north, crossed El Río de Nuestra Señora de Dolores[67] and halted on its northern edge. This river rises from La Sierra de la Plata's northern flank, runs southwest to this place, and from here makes a turn. It is a bit smaller than El Río del Norte around this time of year. Today a little more than eight leagues and a half.[68]

August 13

On the 13th we made camp, both to allow the padre to improve some more in order to go ahead, and to take a bearing on the polar elevation of this site and meadow of El Río de los Dolores, where we found ourselves. The bearing was taken by the sun, and we saw that we were at 38° 13 1/2′ latitude.[69] Here there is everything that a good settlement needs for its establishment and maintenance as regards irrigable lands, pasturage, timber, and firewood. Upon an elevation on the river's south side, there was in ancient times a small settlement of the same type as those of the Indians of New Mexico, as the ruins

67. "Our Lady of Sorrows." Today called simply the Dolores River. The campsite was located very near the present-day site of Dolores, Colorado. It was probably right at the point where the Dolores River turns to the north.

68. Over 22 miles. The travel was easy going over mostly flat terrain, and it is easy to see why they could cover that distance on that day.

69. Their calculation is too high. They were actually at 37° 29′ N.

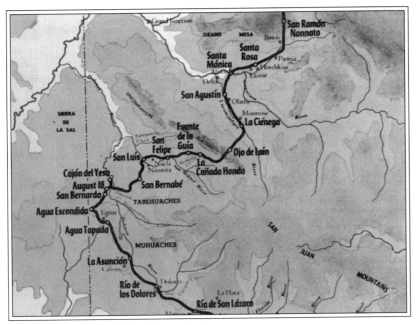

RÍO DE SAN LÁZARO TO SAN RAMÓN
AUGUST 12–AUGUST 31

which we purposely inspected show.[70] Padre Fray Francisco Atanasio got better, and we decided to continue our journey the following day.

August 14

On the 14th we set out from the meadow and Río de Dolores toward the north, and after a quarter league of travel we continued northwest for one league and to the northwest by west for five leagues over a rather troublesome stretch of sagebrush. We entered a tall and craggy canyon and, after going through it two leagues to the north, we arrived a second time at El Río de Dolores, which already here runs northwest. We crossed it twice within a brief space and halted by its western edge,

70. In this vicinity today (June 1975) an Anasazi site called "The Escalante Ruin" is being stabilized and a museum is being constructed by the U.S. Bureau of Land Management. This may or may not be the one mentioned in the journal.

calling the stopping-point, which is a brief meadow of good pasturage, La Asunción de Nuestra Señora.[71]

This afternoon we were overtaken by a *coyote* and a *genízaro* from Abiquiú, the first Felipe and the second Juan Domingo by name.[72] So as to wander among the heathens, they had run away without the permission of their masters of that pueblo, with the desire of accompanying us as their excuse. We had no use for them, but, to forestall the mischief which either through their ignorance or through their malice they might do by wandering any further among the Yutas if we insisted on their going back, we took them on as companions. Today eight leagues and a quarter.[73]

August 15

On the 15th we set out from La Asunción (on El Río de Dolores) through a canyon of some ruggedness and rock, along which we traveled a quarter league to the west-northwest. We then took to the northwest and, after a little less than a league and a half of travel, turned north-northwest and went over a sagebrush stretch of good and almost level terrain for a little more than three leagues. We turned one league northwest again and, after going another two and a half west and over the trail which, of the two into which it splits, swerves farthest from the river—the one we had been following since La Asunción—we paused to rest in a small arroyo which the guides thought had water; but we found it completely dry.[74]

We did not know if there would be another adequate water source in this direction, and at a suitable distance for reaching it today, and so

71. "The Ascension of Our Lady." This campsite was located on the west bank just opposite where Narriguinnep Creek enters the Dolores River east of Cahone, Colorado (37° 34′ N). There is a small level place here which would have provided the necessary forage for the animals, and firewood would have been no problem.

72. Felipe and Juan Domingo were *genizaros*. In New Mexico a *genizaro* designated a non-Pueblo Indian living in more or less Spanish fashion. Some of them were captives ransomed from the nomadic tribes, and their mixed New Mexico–born descendants inherited the designation. Others were Pueblo Indians who had been expelled from the home village for being overly adaptive to Hispanic culture. In a word, detribalized Indians. A *coyote* was a person of mixed Indian and Spanish parentage—a *mestizo*.

73. About 21.7 miles.

74. Across the Dolores from the confluence with the Narraguinnep Creek, a small canyon runs northwest-southeast. They probably went up this canyon for about 3/4 mile to reach the high land and passed just east of present-day Cahone. They passed just east of Dove Creek, Colorado. It is impossible to determine the exact arroyo in which they stopped for a siesta and sent men forward in search of water.

we ordered a reconnaissance of what we were to travel this afternoon. One was found, but so scanty that it sufficed for the people only and not for the horse herds. It was covered up with rocks and wood, evidently on purpose. It consists of permanent water, not too tasty. Perhaps the Yutas covered it up because of some misfortune that overtook them at this place, for, according to what was told us by some of the companions who have traveled among them, this is what they are accustomed to do in such cases. In the afternoon we set out again and, after two leagues of travel northwest and one-half north, we arrived at the water source mentioned, which we named La Agua Tapada.[75] Today nine leagues and three-quarters.[76]

August 16

On the 16th we discovered more than half of the horses missing, since, having had no water, they strayed away looking for it and found it near the trail halfway back on yesterday's march. They made their appearance, arriving when it was already late. For this reason we left La Agua Tapada at half past ten in the morning, taking a little-used trail which we figured would last us until we again reached El Río de Dolores, which we intended to follow. However, after we had traveled over it for two leagues to the northwest and a league and a half west, it played out on us because the ground was very loose and it had been obliterated by the rains. From here we took to the northwest; at a quarter of a league we entered a canyon, wide at its mouth, where we found a well-used trail (*camino*). We followed it and, after another quarter league of traveling northward, we found a water source that appeared to us sufficient for the people and the horse herds and which, for its lying hidden on the eastern side within a dense wood of piñon and juniper, we called La Agua Escondida.[77] No further directions are given because the trail goes right to it.

Two waterholes were made so that the horse herds could drink, and they drank all of it, although not quite enough to be sated

75. "The Covered Water." It is impossible to determine the exact location of this "covered pool" where they camped for the night. It was probably just west of Colorado State Highway 141 and almost directly south of Egnar, Colorado. The Agua Tapada campsite was perhaps a pool formed at the end of an arroyo and possibly impounded by a small earthen dam built by the Utes. Perhaps they covered it to prevent evaporation and thus have a water supply on the high land, thereby not having to go all the way down to the Dolores River.

76. Just over 25.5 miles.

77. "The Hidden Water."

altogether. While we were reconnoitering the terrain on either side in order to proceed this afternoon, Don Bernardo Miera set out all alone through the said canyon without our seeing him. And so, while impelled to continue the day's march, we halted and sent another companion to bring him back before he could get lost; but he had gone so far ahead that they did not arrive until after midnight at the place where the rest of us were waiting, extremely worried over the two's delay. They said that they had arrived through the canyon at El Río de Dolores, and that in the intervening space there was no more than a difficult but improvable stretch for getting through. This made us decide to continue through here the next day. Today four leagues.[78]

August 17

On the 17th we set out from La Agua Escondida, and about half past three in the afternoon we arrived a third time at El Río de Dolores, having traveled along the entire canyon[79] and its many turns for seven leagues to the north, which in a straight line must be four or five at the most. The canyon we named El Laberinto de Miera[80] because of the varied and pleasing scenery of rock cliffs which it has on either side and which, for being so lofty and craggy at the turns, makes the exit seem all the more difficult the farther one advances—and because Don Bernardo Miera was the first one to go through it. It is negotiable all the way and not too troublesome for the horse herds, except one passage which can be easily improved.

On reaching the river we saw quite recent tracks of Yutas,[81] from which we figured there was an encampment of theirs nearby. And, weighing the fact that if they had seen us and we did not make advances toward them they might suspect some mischief on our part, the fear of which would alarm them, and that one of them might be able to guide us or furnish us with some hints for continuing our journey with less difficulty and hardship than the one we were now experiencing—

---

78. Ten and one-half miles.
79. Summit Canyon.
80. "Miera's Labyrinth." Named after Don Bernardo Miera y Pacheco, the retired military captain who accompanied the expedition as cartographer.
81. The Spaniards referred to the present-day Ute Indians as the Yutas.

for none of our companions knew the water sources and terrain ahead—we decided to seek them out.[82]

As soon as we halted by a bend of the river, which we named San Bernardo,[83] Padre Fray Francisco set forth, accompanied by Andrés Muñiz the interpreter and Don Juan Pedro Cisneros, following the tracks upstream for about three leagues. They ascertained that they were Tabehuachi Yutas[84] but could not find them, after having gone as far as the point where the little Río de las Paralíticas[85] (so named because the first of our own to see it found in an encampment by its edge three female Yutas with the infirmity of this name) separates the Tabehuachi Yutas from the Muhuachi[86] ones, the latter living to the south and the others to the north. Today seven leagues, which in a straight line would be four to the north.[87]

August 18

On the 18th two of the companions set out early to study a way by which we could get out of the river's box channel, which here has tall and very rocky mesas on either side, so as not to get too far away from it for as long as it did not change direction, which is north here, nor stray too far off for lack of water and pasturage. No way was found by which to get out without going through the river's box channel, in which, because of so much rock and the necessity of having to cross it many times, we feared that our mounts would wear out their hooves. Leaving El Ancón de San Bernardo, we went one league downstream toward the north and halted[88] so that they could go on to survey more than what they had traveled during the morning. They returned about eight in the morning, saying that only through the river's box channel

82. The entrada had reached the limit of any member's experience. Therefore, they hoped to enlist the aid of the local inhabitants.

83. This campsite is on the Dolores River in Summit Canyon. Disappointment Valley opens up immediately east of the campsite. At the present time there is considerable mining activity opposite Summit Canyon.

84. The Taviwatsiu.

85. Paralysis River—so named, they said, because of the three Indian women seen on its banks who were suffering some form of paralysis. They were probably on present-day Disappointment Creek.

86. Today the Mowatei Indians of the Ute.

87. Today, because of the many twists and turns, they calculated that they traveled over 18 miles, but which, if they could have gone in a straight line, would have been only 10.5 miles.

88. From the mouth of Summit Canyon they proceeded almost due north along the Dolores River and camped at the mouth of McIntyre Canyon.

could we get out, although with difficulty, from this impassable mass of mesas. And so we decided to proceed through the river's box channel. Today one league[89] north.

August 19

On the 19th we continued downstream[90] and, after going with no little difficulty one league to the northeast and another northwest, we halted by another bend of the river so that, after the mounts had drunk, we might be able to leave it and follow a path which went northwest, here taking the river northward should the terrain's roughness allow us to do so. In the meantime, one of the companions went to find out if this path was negotiable up to where one passed the chain of high and rocky mesas over which we intended to cross, since by now the river's box channel was impassable. It was discovered that the path did not go over passable ground in that northwesterly direction. Another footpath or trail was found going southwest; but, even though it was gone over for a long distance during which it presented no obstacle, we did not risk following it because, farther ahead of what had been inspected, high mesas and canyons could be seen where we could again hem ourselves in and find ourselves forced to backtrack.

Over and above this, the great aridness of the surroundings already seen made us believe that whatever rainwater pools and even small springs of running water that might be encountered hereabouts would turn out to be completely dry. We conferred with the companions who had journeyed through this region as to which direction we should take in order to forestall so many difficulties, and each one had a different opinion. Therefore, finding ourselves in this quandary, not knowing if we could follow the path mentioned or if it was better to backtrack a little and take the trail which goes to the Sabuagana Yutas,[91] we put our trust in God and our will in that of His most holy Majesty; then, after begging the intercession of our thrice-holy patron saints that God might direct us through where it would be more conducive to His most holy service, we cast lots between those two trails and drew that of the Sabuaganas. This one we decided to follow until we reached them.

We took a bearing by the sun's position at this site, which we

89. That is, 2.63 miles.
90. That is, down the Dolores River.
91. The Mowataviwatsiu Utes.

named El Cajón del Yeso[92] for there being some [gypsum] at a nearby mesa, and found ourselves at 39° 6′ latitude.[93] Today two leagues.[94]

<h2 style="text-align:center">August 20</h2>

On the 20th we got out of El Cajón del Yeso, backtracking one league to the southeast; we crossed the river again,[95] east-northeast of which about a quarter league away we saw, on some small mounts, outcroppings of very good transparent gypsum. After crossing the river we entered a very wide ravine, and over a well-beaten trail which goes toward the foot of a tall mesa we traveled three leagues to the east-northeast. Then, at the importunities of Don Bernardo Miera, who did not favor following this course, Andrés the interpreter took us over a high rough incline, so rocky that we expected to find ourselves forced to backtrack from halfway up, for the mounts were being so much abused that many of them were marking the spoor on the stones with the blood which these were drawing from their hind and fore feet. We climbed it with the most trying labor and at the end of several north-bound hours, after having gone about a quarter league in the ascent, we traveled a mile northwest atop the crest. And from here we saw that the trail went along the base of this mesa and over good and entirely level terrain.

In the descent, which is extensive and without stone, we went north for more than three-quarters of a league. We continued northeast a little more than a league over a sagebrush stretch where there was a lot of small prickly pear cactus,[96] and to avoid the trouble which this caused the mounts we entered the box channel of an arroyo; then, after going through it for a league to the east, we unexpectedly came upon a

---

92. Following the Dolores River, they passed Steamboat Hill and Grassy Hill and camped where the Little Gypsum Valley opens onto the Dolores, at the south end of Andy's Mesa. This camp marked a major change in plans for the expedition because of the casting of lots and the determination to take the trail that would lead them to the Sabuagana Utes in a general east-northeast direction. Apparently casting lots was a favorite decision-making device. On October 11 another lot was cast which affected the entire outcome of the expedition.

93. They were perhaps closer to 37° 30′. Their calculations were considerably off at this point. Disappointment Creek enters the Dolores at 38° 1′ 30″, with the Little Gypsum Canyon and Creek some 7′ farther north. This reading was probably taken at 38° 8′ 30″.

94. About 5 1/4 miles.

95. Still on the Dolores River.

96. The nopal is commonly called *tunas* in the Southwest. The Anglos called this the prickly pear cactus.

plenteous source of good water, consisting of that which banks up when it rains and of some from a tiny spring. This we named San Bernabé.[97] As the trails and the ruins of huts hereabouts indicate, it is a Yuta camping site, and to it comes the trail we had left on climbing that impassable incline. We halted here even though the pasturage is not very abundant, after having traveled six leagues[98] today (not counting the backtracking).

August 21

On the 21st we set out from the El Aguaje de San Bernabé and, through the canyon where it is situated at its southern end, we traveled north four leagues of very good terrain and some difficult stretches. Midway in the canyon there are good waterholes, and almost at the end for the space of a quarter league as much water flows as that coming from a middling spring. After passing through this canyon we went one league northwest, a little less, over a level stretch of sagebrush. We entered another canyon,[99] as bad for traveling as the foregoing was, and, after going through it one league to the north, we reached El Río de San Pedro[100] and halted in a small meadow it has here, naming it El Paraje de San Luis.[101] Today six leagues.[102]

August 22

On the 22nd we left El Paraje de San Luis, crossed the river, went up a rather high and steep incline, but not too rocky, and started over an extensive mesa which is like a piece off La Sierra de los Tabehuachis.[103] We went over it northeast for two leagues, east-northeast for more

97. They were southeast of Spectacle Reservoir, from which they entered the west fork of Dry Creek Canyon and camped on a Ute camping site. They refer to this later as "El Aguaje de San Bernabé," or a "waterhole."

98. About 15 3/4 miles.

99. The southeastern end of Paradox Valley.

100. "Saint Peter's River." Today called the San Miguel River (Saint Michael).

101. This campsite was located northwest of Naturita, Colorado, in a meadow on the west side of the San Miguel River at about the junction of present-day Colorado State Highways 141 and 90.

102. There is considerable discrepancy between the six leagues (15 3/4 miles) reported in the journal and the distance between the campsites of San Bernabé and San Luis. The distance would appear to be no more than 3 1/2–4 leagues instead of 6. Perhaps the windings of Dry Creek, which they followed to the San Miguel (Río de San Pedro), threw off their calculations.

103. The Uncompahgre Plateau.

than half a league, east-southeast for another half, and descended the mesa down another steep but short incline, and it is the one which Don Juan María de Ribera[104] in his diary dwells on as being very trying. Then we traveled along the edge of El Río de San Pedro (upstream) for a league toward the northeast. We paused for a rest, and they went on to reconnoiter what we were to travel in the afternoon—by getting away from the river now if there was a water source handy, and if not, the following day. Those who had gone out for this purpose returned late, and so we slept [*overwritten*: ended the march] at this spot, which we named San Felipe.[105] Today four leagues.[106]

August 23

On the 23rd we left El Paraje de San Felipe (on El Río de San Pedro), went up a hill, and along the foot of La Sierra de los Tabehuachis (thus called for being inhabited by the Yutas of this name) we traveled for four leagues, which, because of the turns we made, would be two east from San Felipe. We already had left the said Río de San Pedro, which rises in La Sierra de las Grullas, at its small branch which continues north after the one called Sierra de la Plata and flows northwest and west until it joins the Dolores near the small Sierra de la Sal[107]— so called for there being salt beds next to it from which, as they

104. In 1765 he headed an expedition from Santa Fe to investigate the existence of silver mines reported in the La Plata Mountains and on that trip explored and traded at least as far as the present Gunnison River. Don Joaquín Laín and Andrés Muñiz, interpreters and guides with the Domínguez-Escalante party, had previously accompanied Rivera on his explorations. Rivera subsequently made two and possibly more expeditions into this section of Colorado, apparently penetrating for a considerable distance beyond the Gunnison River, for the journal notes that two of Rivera's companions, Pedro Mora and Gregorio Sandoval, on one of these expeditions thought they had traveled as far as the great Tizón (Colorado) River. As a result of Rivera's trips other expeditions traveled into this region for the purpose of prospecting for precious metals and trading with the Indians. (See Herbert S. Auerbach, *Escalante's Journal*, p. 42.) Professor Donald Cutter of the University of New Mexico has located the Rivera journals of these expeditions into Southwestern Colorado in the Servicio Histórico Militar, Madrid, Spain.

105. On San Miguel River, just west of where Colorado State Highway 90 goes today and not far from the electric generating plant on the river. They passed through the site of the present town of Nucla and reached the San Miguel at about the site of the substation and continued along the river to the campsite of San Felipe (Saint Philip).

106. Ten and a half miles.

107. The La Sal Mountains.

informed us, the Yutas hereabouts provide themselves. It is a medium-sized river.

We stopped to rest near a small source of ever-flowing water coming down from the sierra and on a level sagebrush stretch, which has a narrow valley with good pasturage at its southern end and forming ahead of it something like a low ridge. On top of this are the ruins of a small and ancient pueblo,[108] the houses of which seem to have been made of the stone with which the Tabehuachi Yutas have fashioned a weak and crude rampart. Here once more we found the mounts some pasturage, which had become scarce since El Paraje de la Asunción by El Río de Dolores until today, for the earth was scorched and dry enough to show that no rain had fallen all summer.

It started to rain by afternoon and ceased within a little more than an hour, and we continued our day's march by ascending La Sierra de los Tabehuachis along a high hill, which was ruggedly steep in places; then, after one league of travel to the northeast and another to the east, we were overtaken by a Tabehuachi Yuta, who was the first one we had seen in all that we had traveled until now (since the first day's march from El Pueblo de Abiquiú, when we encountered two others). In order to talk with him at leisure, we halted near the beginning of the water source where we had rested, and here we named it La Fuente de la Guía.[109] We gave him something to eat and to smoke, and afterward through the interpreter we asked him various questions about the land ahead, the rivers, and their course. We also asked him where the Tabehuachis, Muhuachis, and Sabuaganas were.

At first he denied knowing anything, even the country where he lived. However, after he had lost some of the fear and suspicion with which he conversed with us, he said that the Sabuaganas were all in their own country and that soon we would be meeting them; that the Tabehuachis wandered scattered about throughout this sierra and its surroundings; that the rivers, from the San Pedro to the San Rafael inclusive, flow into the Dolores, and the latter joins with the Navajo. We suggested to him that he might want to guide us as far as the encampment of a Sabuagana chieftain who our interpreter and others said was

108. This ruin has not been identified by modern-day researchers.
109. Cottonwood Creek is probably the best permanent water in the area because of the area it drains; they went generally northeast and east from Cottonwood Creek and then reached it again near its source and camped there. *La Fuente de la Guia* means "the guide's fountain," or "the guide's source" of the stream—in other words, a "spring."

very fond of the Spaniards and knew much of the country. He consented on condition that we wait for him until next day in the afternoon; we agreed to wait for him, both to acquire him as a guide and lest he came to suspect something of us which would disturb him and the rest. Today six leagues.[110]

August 24

On the 24th, before twelve, the said Yuta arrived where we were waiting for him—with his family, two other women, and five children, two of these at the breast and three from eight to ten years of age, all of good features and very friendly. They thought we were here to trade, and so they brought cured deerskins and other things to barter. Among these they had raisins of black *manzanita*, about which we already spoke at the beginning of this diary and which are very much like those of small grapes, and very tasty. We gave them to understand, although they did not wholly believe it, that we were not here for what they thought, or carried goods for trading. And lest they took us for scouts intending to conquer their land after we had seen it, and hence impede our progress—judging within ourselves that a report from the Cosninas about the trip made by the Reverend Padre Fray Francisco Garcés[111] might have passed on to the Payuchi Yutaś,[112] and from the latter to the rest—we said that a certain padre, a brother of ours, had come to Cosnina[113] and Moqui[114] and that from here he had gone back to Cosnina.

With this they were allayed, fully sharing in our worry, and said that they had not received any news concerning said padre. We fed them all, and our guide's wife presented us with a bit of jerked deer meat and two dishes of raisin or dried *Manzanita*, and we returned her the favor with flour. After midday we gave the Yuta what he requested for leading us, which were two big all-purpose knives and sixteen strings of white glass beads. These he turned over to his wife, who, along with the other women, went off to their camps at the time we set

110. About 15 3/4 miles.

111. Refers to Fray Francisco Garcés' report of his expedition to Hopi from the mouth of the Colorado River, which he wrote to the Reverend Father Minister of Zuni (Vélez de Escalante) from the village of Oraibi on July 3, 1776, and which was forwarded to Domínguez and Escalante in Santa Fe by Fray Mariano Rosete in Zuni on July 6, 1776. These letters are in Adams and Chavez, *Missions*, pp. 281–86.

112. The Southern Paiute Indians.

113. The Havasupai Indians.

114. The Hopi Indians.

out from La Fuente de la Guía with him (whom we began calling Atanasio from here on.)[115]

We traveled along the sierra's flank for half a league to the east,
another half east-southeast, and a quarter league southeast. We turned
east again, leaving a path which goes to the southeast as it takes off
from the one we were following; and after going three-quarters of a
league, one-quarter southeast and two east, we stopped in a narrow
valley, the descent and ascent of which are very steep but not difficult.
For this reason we called it La Cañada Honda.[116] In it there is a copious
spring of good water, much firewood, and abundant pasturage for the
mounts. Today two leagues.[117]

August 25

On the 25th we set out from La Cañada Honda toward the east and
traveled half a league through dense clumps of scruboak; we swung to
the southeast over less encumbered terrain and went along the same
path for three leagues and a half; then, having gone another half toward the east, we now began crossing the sierra in a northeasterly direction, and at the end of a league and a half of good terrain, now un-
encumbered and without any laborious slope, we reached its top. It is
an eminence of very good pastures and of pleasant scenery due to the
thickets and beautiful poplar groves, briefly spaced from one another,
which it bears. There are three paths here, and we followed the one
going northeast. Having gone a league and a half in this direction, we
halted while still on the northern flank of the sierra and by a copious
spring of good water that we named El Ojo de Laín,[118] which comes out
about six ordinary paces east from the path. Before any repast could be
prepared, which we needed badly enough all along, a full heavy downpour fell. Today seven leagues and a half.[119]

115. It appears that they named their Indian guides after members of the expedi-
tionary party: Atanasio after Fray Atanasio Domínguez, Silvestre after Fray Silvestre
Vélez de Escalante, and Joaquín after Don Joaquín Laín.

116. "The Deep Valley." Across the Uncompahgre Plateau they came to Red Canyon, a very deep one, and descended its steep northern end and camped there on the
branch of Horsefly Creek, which runs through the canyon.

117. Slightly over five miles.

118. "Laín Springs." Named after Don Joaquín Laín of Santa Fe, a member of the
expedition. Skirting the highlands along Horsefly Creek, they turned northeast at
Johnson Spring. There are numerous springs in the vicinity and it is impossible to determine which one was the Ojo de Laín.

119. Nineteen and three-quarters miles.

August 26

On the 26th we set out from El Ojo de Laín toward the northeast and traveled one league. Here the path we were following splits in two, one toward the east-northeast and the other toward the northeast. This one we followed, and after going two leagues and a half northeast we finished descending the sierra and came upon the banks and meadows of El Río de San Francisco[120]—among the Yutas called Ancapagari[121] (which, according to our interpreter, means Red Lake), because they say that near its source there is a spring of red-colored water, hot and ill-tasting. On this river meadow, which is large and very level, there is a very wide and well-beaten trail. We went along it downstream for a league and a half northeast and halted next to a big marsh greatly abounding in pasturage, which we named La Ciénega de San Francisco.[122] Today five leagues.[123]

DESCRIPTION OF THE SIERRAS SEEN THUS FAR[124]

The one of La Grulla and of La Plata begins near the site called El Cobre and adjacent to the now-abandoned settlement. It runs almost northwest from the place where it starts and, about the seventy leagues there must be from Santa Fe, it comes to a point looking west-southwest and is the one they call Sierra de la Plata. From here it runs northnortheast, turning northward just before La Sierra de los Tabehuachis up to the other small one called Venado Alazán, which is where it ends on the northern side. Along the east side, according to reports, it joins that of El Almagre and La Sierra Blanca. To the west-southwest by west from the point of La Plata, about thirty leagues, another small sierra called El Dátil can be seen. This sierra sheds westward all the rivers we have crossed up until now, and the ones ahead up to the one of San Rafael inclusive.

La Sierra de los Tabehuachis, which we have finished crossing, runs toward the north; it must be about thirty leagues in length, and where we crossed over it eight or ten in width. It abounds with good pasturages and is very moist and has good lands for farming without irrigation.

120. The Uncompahgre River.
121. The Uncompahgre River.
122. "The Marsh of St. Francis." This is on the Uncompahgre River where Colorado State Highway 550 crosses the river. It is near the present Ute Tribal Museum.
123. About 13 miles.
124. See the glossary or earlier footnotes for modern names of these features where it has been possible to identify them.

It abundantly produces piñon, ponderosa pine, spruce, scruboak, various kinds of wild fruit, and flax in some places. On it deer and roe and other animals breed, and certain chicken fowl the size and shape of the common domestic ones, from which they differ in not having combs. Their flesh is very tasty. About twenty leagues to the west of this sierra is the one of La Sal, which likewise appears small. To the west-southwest, a matter of four leagues or so, another one can be seen, which they call La Sierra de Abajo.

The said Río de San Francisco is medium sized and a bit larger than the Dolores. It is composed of several rivulets which come down from the western flank of La Sierra de las Grullas and run northwest, according to what we saw. Here it has a meadow of good land for farming with the help of irrigation. It must be three leagues in size. There is all the rest needed for establishing a good settlement on it. Northeast of this meadow there is a chain of small mounts and hills of a leaden color crowned with yellow ochre earth.

August 27

On the 27th we set out from La Ciénega de San Francisco, downstream and heading northwest. At a short distance we met a Yuta, called the Left-handed, with his family. We tarried a good while with him, and after a lengthy conversation drew forth nothing more useful than that we had suffered from the sun's heat, which was indeed very fiery all the while the talk lasted. We continued our day's march through the meadow and, after trekking two leagues and a half to the northeast, crossed the river and dense leafy grove of poplars and other trees which its banks bear hereabouts. We went up a small incline, entered a plain of no pasturage but of very minute stone and, after going all the way downstream for three and a half leagues northwest, halted on another meadow of the same river, which we named San Agustín.[125] It is large and has on either side of it abundant pastures and a great deal of black poplar. Today six leagues.[126]

125. The Uncompahgre River. They traveled along the west bank of the Uncompahgre to the northwest past the present site of Montrose, Colorado. They crossed the river some six miles northwest of La Cienega campsite and marched up the east bank from that point. The probable San Agustin campsite is at the point where the Uncompahgre River splits into several branches, making a broad meadow. It is approximately two miles north of Olathe, Colorado, 38° 36′ 30″.

126. Fifteen and three-quarters miles.

Farther down, and about four leagues to the north of this Vega de San Agustín, this river joins another, larger one, named San Xavier[127] by our own, and river of the Tomichi by the Yutas. To these two rivers, already joined together, there came Don Juan María de Ribera in the year of '65, crossing the same Sierra de los Tabehuachis, on the top of which is the site he named El Purgatorio,[128] according to the indications he gives in his itinerary.

The meadow where he halted in order to ford the river—and where they say he carved on a poplar sapling a cross, the letters spelling his name and the expedition's year—is situated almost near the same juncture on the southern side, as we were assured by our interpreter, Andrés Muñiz, who came with the said Don Juan María in the year mentioned as far as La Sierra de los Tabehuachis. He said that, although he had stayed three days' marches behind on this side of the river at that time when he came along its edge this past year of '75 with Pedro Mora and Gregorio Sandoval—who had accompanied Don Juan María throughout the entire expedition mentioned—they said that they had reached it then and from it had started their return, they alone having crossed it when they were sent by the said Don Juan María to look for Yutas on the side opposite the meadow where they stopped and from where they came back—and so, that this was the one which they then judged to be the great Río del Tizón.[129]

August 28

On the 28th we set out northward from La Vega de San Agustín, already leaving El Río de San Francisco, and after half a league of travel we continued three leagues and a half north-northeast over loose dirt and without stone and arrived at the already mentioned Río de San Francisco Xavier[130] (among the people, San Xavier)—Tomichi by another name—which is made up of four little rivers coming down from the northernmost point (of La Sierra de la Grulla). It is as bounteous in

127. The Uncompahgre River joins a larger one named Río de San Xavier by the Spaniards and Tomichi by the Utes. Today it is known as the Gunnison River.

128. The El Purgatorio of Juan María de Ribera is at the confluence of the Uncompahgre and the Gunnison rivers, now just below Delta, Colorado.

129. The Colorado River. Called the Tizón because the Indians on the lower river carried *tizones*, or firebrands, with them in winter to keep warm. They were not, of course, at that time on the Colorado River, or the Tizón, as they speculated.

130. The Gunnison River. The explorers have given it two names now: Río de San Xavier or Río de San Francisco Xavier.

water as El Norte, runs west, and at the western point of La Sierra del
Venado Alazán[131] it joins the San Francisco, as we already said. Its banks
hereabouts are very sparse in pasturage.

By a bend of it, where we found some pasture for the mounts and
named it Santa Mónica,[132] we stopped today with the intention of rest-
ing awhile and continuing upstream until we came upon some encampments of Sabuaganas, which yesterday we heard were around
here, and in them some Indians from among the Timpanogotzis, or
Lagunas,[133] into whose country we were already planning to go. But after pondering the detour we would have to make in going farther upstream and in this direction—that our mounts would be badly over-
taxed, and that we would necessarily have to use up much of the
provisions in going to their habitations—we agreed on sending the interpreter with the guide Atanasio to summon them and see if anyone
of them or of the Lagunas wanted to lead us, while we were to pay him
for as far as he knew. They went over, and we remained waiting for
them in Santa Mónica. Today four leagues.[134] The latitude of this place
was taken by the sun's meridian, and it is 39° 13′ 29″ [22″].[135]

August 29

On the 29th, about ten in the morning, five Sabuagana Yutas, yelling
loudly, let themselves be seen on top of some hills on the other side. We
figured them to be those whom we had sent to be sought out, but as
soon as they arrived where we were we realized that they were not from
among those summoned. We gave them wherewith to eat and smoke,
but after a long parley—its subject being the quarrels they had been

131. "The Mountain of the Sorrel-Colored Deer." They had probably seen many
deer in this area.
132. Located in the Gunnison Valley about one-half mile east of Austin, Colorado.
It is at the northwest corner of Smith's Mountain on the south bank of the Gunnison
River.
133. Various spellings in the journal. The Lagunas are now Uintah Utes. *Timpanogotzis* appears to be an Aztecan rendition of a Ute name. According to George Stewart it would seem to be derived from an Old Ute name for the mountain now called
Timpanogos. Not having gender, the name seems to mean "the stone person" or
"stone one" and refers to the image of a reclining human being formed by the ridges
of the mountain Timpanogos.
134. Ten and a half miles.
135. Still too high. They were closer to 38° 45′ at this point.

having this summer with the Yamparica Comanches[136]—we could not draw out of them anything useful for our plan, because theirs was to fill us with fear by exaggerating the danger to which we were exposing ourselves of being killed by the Comanches if we continued on our course. We refuted the validity of these pretenses, by which they were trying to stop us from going ahead, by telling them that our God, who is everyone's, would defend us if we should happen to run into these foes.

August 30

On the 30th in the morning the interpreter Andrés and the guide Atanasio arrived with five Sabuaganas and one Laguna. After we had regaled them with plenty of food and tobacco, we informed them of our purpose, which was to pass on to the pueblo or pueblos of the Lagunas (the Yutas had told us that the Lagunas dwelt in pueblos like those of New Mexico), telling them that, since they were our friends, they should give us a good guide who would conduct us as far as these peoples and that we would pay him to his satisfaction. They replied that to go to the place we were trying to reach there was no other trail than the one passing through the midst of the Comanches and that these would impede our passage and even deprive us of our lives—and finally that none of them knew the country between here and the Lagunas. This they repeated many times, insisting that we had to turn back from here. We tried to convince them, first by arguing and then by cajoling, so as not to displease them. Then we showed the Laguna a woolen blanket, a big all-purpose knife, and white glass beads, telling him this is what we were giving him so that he would accompany us and serve us as a guide all the way to his country. He agreed, and the things mentioned were turned over to him.

When the Sabuaganas saw this, they quit posing difficulties and now acknowledged that some of them knew the way. Following all this, they strongly insisted on our going over to their encampment, saying that the Laguna did not know the trail by any other way. Well did we know that it was a new ruse to detain us and longer enjoy the kindnesses we were doing them; for to as many as came there—and today they were plenty—we gave them to eat and to smoke. However, so as

136. These are Comanche or Eastern Shoshone, or even possibly a different band of Ute Indians.

not to give them cause for displeasure or lose such a good guide as we had acquired, we yielded and agreed to go over.

This afternoon we left Santa Mónica, crossed El Río de San Xavier,[137] in which the water reached the mounts well above the shoulder blades, climbed a hill, and, over broken terrain but tractable and without stone, traveled upstream and east-northeast for two leagues; then, after going another two northeast over country not quite as broken up but with some sagebrush, a lot of small prickly pear cactus, and finely ground black lava, we halted at the edge of a little river which we named Santa Rosa.[138] It rises in La Sierra del Venado Alazán, on the southern flank of which we now find ourselves, and enters into that of San Xavier. Here it has a medium-sized meadow of good pasturage and a scenic grove of white poplar and scruboak. Today four leagues.[139] The Sabuaganas and the Laguna spent the night with us.

August 31

On the 31st we set out from El Río de Santa Rosa de Lima toward the northeast, went a league and a half over good country, and arrived at another medium-sized river, which comes down from the same sierra like the previous one and with it enters into the San Xavier, and we named it Río de Santa María,[140] in the leas and bends of which there is all that is needed for the founding and subsistence of two settlements. We went to the northeast four leagues and a half upstream, over those meadows and through the groves which it also has, crossing it once. We turned north, crossed the river again, entered a woods of juniper and a great deal of rock which lasted for about three miles; then we continued by going up La Sierra del Venado Alazán along the slope of a very deep narrow valley, breaking through dense clumps of scruboak; then, after going four leagues northward also, we stopped at a perennial water source, which we named San Ramón Nonato.[141]

One of the Sabuagana Yutas who accompanied us from Santa Mónica today ate with such brutish savagery that we thought he was going to die from overstuffing. On finding himself so sick, he claimed

137. The Gunnison River.
138. Known today as the Leroux Creek. The campsite was on Leroux Creek, some 12 miles from the last campsite.
139. Ten and a half miles.
140. The north fork of the Gunnison River.
141. Located in a meadow one mile north of the confluence of Willow Creek and Hubbard Creek, in Hubbard Canyon.

that the Spaniards had done him harm. This stupid notion caused us a great deal of worry, for we already knew that these barbarians, when they happen to get sick after having eaten what someone else gives them—even if he be from among their own—believe that he damaged them and try to avenge an injury which they never received. But God willed that he recovered, after he vomited some of the great mass he could not digest. Today nine leagues.[142]

142. A little more than 23.5 miles.

✠

SAN RAMÓN–LAS LLAGAS

SEPTEMBER 1–SEPTEMBER 16

September 1

On the 1st of September we set out, headed north from San Ramón, and after going three leagues through small narrow valleys of abundant pastures and thick clumps of scruboak[143] we came upon eighty Yutas, all on good horses and most of them from the encampment to which we were going. They told us that they were going out to hunt, but we figured that they came together like this, either to show off their strength in numbers or to find out if any other Spanish people were coming behind us or if we came alone; for, since they knew from the night before that we were going to their encampment, it was unnatural for almost all of its men to come out at the very time that they knew we were to arrive, unless motivated by what we have just said.

We kept on going with only the Laguna, descended a very steep incline, and came into a very pleasant narrow valley, in which there was a small river[144] and all along its bank a spreading grove of spruces, very tall and straight, among them certain poplars which seem to ape the erectness and height of the pines. Through this narrow valley we traveled eastward for a league and reached the encampment, which had numerous people and must have consisted of thirty tents. We stopped a mile down from it by the edge of the river mentioned, naming the site San Antonio Mártir.[145] Today four leagues[146]—199 [in all].[147]

As soon as we halted, Padre Fray Francisco Atanasio went on to the encampment with Andrés the interpreter to see the chieftain and the

---

143. The party left San Ramón Nonato and ascended Hubbard Creek into Hubbard Park. They encountered the eighty Utes near the present site of the Electric Mountain Hunting Lodge in the north extremity of the part on Electric Mountain on present Grand Mesa.

144. In those days Cow Creek was probably much larger because Overland Reservoir did not impound its waters.

145. This campsite is located where Fawn Creek enters Cow Creek at the 8,600-foot elevation.

146. Ten and a half miles.

147. According to their calculations, they had journeyed over 523 miles since July 29.

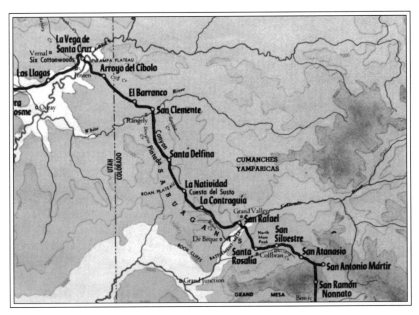

SAN RAMÓN TO LAS LLAGAS, SEPTEMBER 1–SEPTEMBER 16

others who had remained. He went into the chieftain's tent and, after greeting and embracing him and his children, asked him to gather there the people who were on hand. He did so, and when those of either sex who could attend had been assembled, he announced the Gospel to them through the interpreter. All listened with pleasure, and especially six Lagunas who were present, among whom our guide and another Laguna stood out. As soon as the padre began instructing them, the new guide mentioned interrupted them so as to predispose the Sabuaganas as well as his own fellow tribesmen "to believe whatever the padre was telling them because it all was true." In the same way, the other Laguna relayed the pleasure and eagerness with which he heard the news of his eternal salvation.

Among those listening there was one a bit deaf who, not grasping what was being treated, asked what it was the padre was saying. Then this Laguna said: "The padre says that this which he shows us"—it was the image of Christ crucified—"is the one Lord of all, who dwells in the highest part of the skies, and in order to please Him and go to Him one has to be baptized and must beg His forgiveness." He emphasized this idea by beating his breast with his hand—a surprising gesture on his part for his never having seen it made before, either by the padre or by the interpreter. When the padre saw the evident joy with which they heard him, he suggested to the chieftain now in charge of the encampment that if, after he had conferred with his people, they would accept Christianity we would come to instruct them and set them in a way of living that would lead to baptism. He replied that he would propose it to his people, but he did not return all afternoon to provide further cause whereon to base a likely hope of their accepting the proposal.

Filled with joy by the open declaration of the Lagunas mentioned, the padre asked how the latter one was called (the guide we had already named Silvestre),[148] and on learning that they called him Red Bear he instructed them all by explaining to them the difference existing between men and brutes, the purpose for which either of them were created, and the wrong thing they did in naming themselves after wild beasts—thus placing themselves on a par with them, and even below them. Promptly he told the Laguna to call himself Francisco from then on. When the rest saw this, they began repeating this name, although with difficulty, the Laguna joyfully pleased for being so named.

It also happened that when the padre addressed as chief the one who, as already said, was in charge of the encampment, he replied that he was not it and that the real chief was a fine-looking youth who was present; and when the padre asked him if he [the youth] was married, he answered that he was and that he had two wives. This embarrassed the said youth (whom the other had done the honor of pointing out for his being the brother of a greatly revered chieftain among the Sabuaganas named Yamputzi), and he tried to make out that he had only one wife. From this it can be inferred that these barbarians are aware or cognizant of the repuganance inherent in having multiple wives at one and the same time. From here the padre grasped the opportunity to instruct them on this point, and to exhort them not to have more than one.

When this was all over, some jerked bison meat was bought from them, they being paid for it with white beads, and they were asked if they wanted to exchange some horses for other now hoofsore ones that

148. Silvestre would guide the party to present Utah Valley and Utah Lake. The debt to this Indian guide as well as to others engaged along the trail was considerable. Silvestre knew the trail well and thus prevented the padres from making misjudgments as to the route to be followed.

we brought along. They replied that they would exchange them later in the afternoon. This done, the padre came back to the king's camp.[149]

A little before sundown the chief, some very old men, and many of the others came to where we were. They began trying to persuade us to turn back from here, exaggerating anew and with greater effort the hardships and perils to which we were exposing ourselves by going ahead, saying for certain that the Comanches would not let us do so— and that they did not tell us this to stop us from going as far as we wanted, but because they esteemed us highly. We acknowledged this token and told them that the one God whom we worshiped would expedite everything for us and would defend us, not only from the Comanches but also from all others who might intend to do us harm, and that we feared not a thing of what they were bringing up because we were certain that His Majesty was on our side.

Seeing that their pretexts were of no avail, they said that since we wished to go ahead without paying heed to what they warned us about we should write to the great chief of the Spaniards (thus they call the lord governor), telling him that we passed through their country, so that, in the event that we had some mishap and did not return, the Spaniards would not think that they had taken our lives. This was a ruse from among some of our own companions, who wanted to turn back or loiter among them. We answered them that we would write to him, and would leave them the letter for the day one of them went to New Mexico and took it along. They replied that they did not offer to take it, that we should send it by one of our own. We told them that none of these could go back or stay among them. Finally, now that they found no other way to hinder our passage without declaring themselves our enemies, they said that if we did not turn back from here they would not make exchanges for the hoofsore horses we had; to this we replied that we would go on even if they made no exchange, because under no circumstances would we turn back without knowing the whereabouts of the padre our brother who had been among the Moquis and Cosninas and might be wandering about lost.

149. The diarists used the word *real* or "king's camp" to refer to their campsites in order to differentiate from the camps or encampments of Indians encountered along the trail. To understand why they used the term *real* it is necessary to put oneself in their shoes and see things as they saw them. They believed they were in fact representing the king on this expedition and would therefore refer to their campsites as literally "the king's camp."

To this they replied, prompted by those of our very own who understood their language and were underhandedly giving us a rough time, that the padres could not get lost because they carried drawn on paper all the lands and routes of travel. They began pressing again, by rehashing all that has been related about our turning back from here. Then, on seeing our unshakeable determination, they repeated that they were urging us not to go ahead because they loved us, but that if we wished to do so they were not stopping us and that in the morning they would exchange the horses. They took their leave well after nightfall, not without hope of overcoming our determination next day, for, as we came to find out, they were assured of it by Felipe—the one from Abiquiú—Andrés the interpreter, and his brother Lucrecio, they being the ones who, either out of fear or because they did not want to go ahead, were secretly prompting the Sabuaganas ever since they learned that they were opposed to our plans.[150] This caused us much grief and very much also what follows.

Ever since La Villa de Santa Fe, we had reminded all of the companions that those who wished to be part of this expedition were not to take along any goods for trading and that those who did not agree to this condition were to stay behind. All agreed not to bring a thing, nor to have any purpose other than the one we had, which was God's glory and the good of souls. For this reason, everything that they requested for their equipment and to leave to their families was rationed out to them. But some of them failed in their promise by secretly carrying some goods we did not see until we were near to the Sabuaganas. And here we charged and begged them all not to engage in commerce, so that the infidels might understand that another motive higher than this one brought us through these parts.

We had just been telling the Sabuaganas that we needed neither arms nor men because we placed all our safety and defense in God's almighty arm, and Andrés our interpreter, with his brother Lucrecio, proved themselves to be such obedient and faithful Christians[151] that they peddled what they secretly brought along and most greedily sought weapons from the infidels, telling them that they badly needed them because they were about to pass through the lands of the Comanches. In this way, to our own sorrow, they betrayed their

---

150. Fathers Domíguez and Escalante will have further trouble with these men.
151. No doubt meant sarcastically.

meager faith or lack of it, and how very unfit they were for ventures of this kind.

September 2

On the 2nd of September, quite early, the same ones assembled in our king's camp, and even more than yesterday afternoon. Again they began pressing the arguments mentioned above, adding another new and grave impediment, for they completely dissuaded the Laguna from his intent of leading us and made him give us back what we had given him for accompanying us to his country. After having argued for more than an hour and a half, without getting the guide to take back what he had received and to keep his word—or them to quit opposing us—we told them with the firmness such an urgency called for that, after the Laguna had willingly agreed to accompany us to his country and they had put up so many obstacles, we clearly knew for certain that it was they who deprived us of the guide and impeded our journey, that we would not turn back no matter how much they tried, that we would go ahead even without a guide, but that if the Laguna did not come with us they should know that from then on we no longer considered them our friends.

Thereupon they lost their self-assurance, and the above-mentioned youth, brother of Chief Yamputzi, addressed the others and said that, since they had granted us passage and the Laguna had agreed to guide us, placing obstacles before us was no longer appropriate and that they should therefore stop talking about this matter. Another one, who was also said to be a chieftain, followed him with the same exhortation. Then all of them told the Laguna that he could no longer refuse to accompany us. He, because of what they had told him before, no longer wanted to. After much urging and coaxing he accepted his pay, although with some reluctance, and agreed to accompany us.

The encampment was already changing location, and they were on the march to where Chief Yamputzi was, at the time we were leaving the painful Paraje de San Antonino Mártir.[152] We did not know what direction to take, because the guide, regretting the deal, did not want to go ahead or show us the way. He stayed behind at the encampment's site with the horse we gave him, under the pretext of looking for a saddle, while we continued along the route the Sabuaganas took, although against our will because we wanted to get away from them. We

---

152. On Cow Creek where Fawn Creek discharges into it.

ordered the interpreter to get him back right away and to try to comfort him. He did so, and, when all the Yutas were gone, the guide now said which way we were to take and sent the interpreter to bring us back to where he had stayed. Here we found him taking leave of his other countrymen who were remaining with the Sabuaganas, and they charged him to conduct us with care, telling him how to apportion the day's marches. Besides the guide Silvestre, here we found another Laguna, still a boy, who wanted to go with us. Since we had not known of his intent, we had not provided a mount for him, and so to avoid further delay Don Joaquín Laín pulled him up hind-saddle on his own.

With utmost pleasure did we leave the route which the encampment was taking, and with the two Lagunas—Silvestre and the lad whom we named Joaquín[153]—pursued our own travel plan and, after tracing back a league toward the west of San Antonino, we took another trail; we traveled less than a league and three-quarters northwest and more than a quarter west-northwest and halted in a short valley of good pastures near a rivulet of good water, which we named San Atanasio.[154] Today we traveled three leagues[155] over good terrain and through a poplar grove and clumps of scruboak but advanced two leagues[156] only. Tonight it rained heavily.

September 3

On the 3rd it rained again very early, and we had to wait for it to stop; then, about eleven, we set out from San Atanasio toward the north. At a quarter of a league we took to the northwest and traveled two leagues and a quarter through a valley of many poplar groves and spruce and very abundant in pasturage and water.[157] We turned north-northwest one league, then northwest somewhat more than a league and three-

153. Joaquín accompanied the party to Utah Lake and then on to Santa Fe. He became greatly attached to the padres and they to him. Even after reaching his people at the lake, Joaquín would not leave the padres and stayed "glued to the padre" and slept by his side. See entry for September 23. He was later baptized in Santa Fe.

154. Undoubtedly named after Father Domínguez (Fray Francisco *Atanasio* Domínguez). Leaving San Antonino Mártir the expedition went up Cow Creek. They crossed over to Dyke Creek over a pass westward of Chimney Rock and camped in the extreme portion of Mule Park on the upper West Muddy Creek.

155. That is, 7.89 miles.

156. Five and a quarter miles.

157. Buzzard Park. They traveled the south face of Bronco Knob at the 9,800-foot level northwest through Wagon Park and Plateau Park and down Plateau Creek to the Meadows. At the west end of the Meadows, Plateau Creek becomes the deep arroyo mentioned.

quarters over good and stoneless terrain, although with some hills, passing through rather troublesome forests of spruce and poplar and clumps of scruboak. We turned north-northwest again for a quarter of a league through a low, narrow valley in which enough water flows to fill two middling furrows; and although it does not continue all through the narrow valley, since it disappears completely in some places, running in spots and in others reappearing in water holes like ponded rainwater, it seems to be perennial because throughout the entire narrow valley there were huts and tiny dwellings, which indicate that it is a camping site for these Yutas. Following the box channel of an arroyo in which said water disappears and reappears along the northern side and to the northwest, we went a league and a half and halted in it almost at the foot of a bluff which the Yutas call Nabuncari,[158] we naming the site San Silvestre.[159] Today seven leagues.[160]

September 4

On the 4th we left San Silvestre and headed northwest, following the same arroyo. At a short distance we turned west-northwest and after two leagues swung northwest again, went up a very high incline leaving the arroyo's box channel toward the south, and traveled another half league among hills of various kinds of broom. We went down to another rivulet which flows into the arroyo mentioned; we crossed it, went up another incline with some rock and piñon growth, and after a quarter league almost west-southwest we crossed it again already joined with the arroyo. Here with tree sections the beavers have constructed ponds so big that they look like a more than medium-sized river at first sight. Then we went west along the southern side and over a sagebrush plain for three-quarters of a league, and we crossed it once more to continue along the other side and leave it to the south.

Having crossed it we took to the west-northwest, passed through a section of piñon growth, and came upon a sagebrush stretch where three Yuta women with a child were preparing the small fruits they had picked for their sustenance in the arroyos and rivulets hereabouts. We

158. Campbell Mountain.
159. Named by the explorers after Father Escalante (Fray *Silvestre* Vélez de Escalante). It appears that the explorers themselves named at least one place after each member of the expedition. The placing of numerous Escalante place-names in Utah came much later. The campsite was located west of the northern peak of Campbell Mountain.
160. Almost 18.5 miles.

went over to talk to them, and right away they offered us their fruits, which were chokecherry, gooseberry, *lemita*, and some of this year's piñon nuts. The gooseberry which grows in these parts is very sour on the bush, but when already exposed to the sun, as these Yuta women had it, it has a very delicious sweet-sour taste. We took up our day's march, and after going a league and a half west-northwest from the rivulet mentioned (crossing another one next to the Yutas, at the exit of which there is a leaning rock about five palms high, shaped like a laundering place on which some horses slipped), we entered a narrow valley or small dale of good pasturage.

Here another trail comes in, the one which from Santa Mónica and Río de San Xavier directly crosses over La Sierra del Venado Alazán—which we finished descending today—and is halfway shorter than the one we have been following. We turned northwest along the narrow valley for a little more than half a league. We went west-northwest once more, and after another half a league, going up and down a rather long and steep but rockless incline, crossed a rivulet of extremely cold water and halted by its edge, naming it and the little valley of good pastures that are here Santa Rosalía.[161] Tonight, and the one before, we were feeling the cold very much. Today six leagues[162]—201 [in all].[163]

September 5

On the 5th we left Santa Rosalía, headed northwest, and went up an incline without troublesome rocks but extremely steep and dangerous when approaching the top, because there are winding turns where the path is no more than a third of a yard wide. The footing is of very loose white dirt, and so it is very easy for some horse to slip; and should it happen to lose its footing it would not be able to keep itself from reaching the level ground below. The ascent must be somewhat more than a quarter league long, counting the half already covered. We descended it through a spreading narrow valley which in places produces nothing but scruboak and chokecherry, and in others ponderosa pine

161. On Jerry Gulch, where a stream of cool water and pasturage existed.
162. Fifteen and three-quarters miles.
163. According to their calculations they had traveled over 528 miles from Santa Fe. They seem to be mixed up. To September 1 they had journeyed 199 leagues, or 523 miles. Now, on September 4, they record 201 leagues in all having been traveled. Actually, since September 1 they had traveled 15 leagues, or 39 miles, making a total of 214 leagues, or 562 miles.

and white poplar; then, after going a little more than four leagues to the northwest, we entered a small wood of juniper while swinging half a league north-northwest, and after a short stretch of sagebrush arrived at a river which our own call San Rafael[164] and the Yutas Red River.

We crossed it and halted by its northern edge on a meadow of good pastures and a middling poplar grove. On this side there is a chain of high mesas which are of white earth from the top down to the middle and from the middle down evenly striated with yellow, white, and not too deeply tinged red ochre. This river carries more water than El Norte; it comes down, according to what they told us, from a great lake which lies in the high Sierra de los Sabuaganas[165] next (toward the north) to La Grulla. Its course along here is to the west-southwest, and it enters the Dolores. At the ford it splits into two branches,[166] and the water reached the mounts above the shoulder blades. Some which crossed farther up from the ford swam in places. Everywhere we could see, the river has many rocks, and big ones; hence, whenever some party should find it necessary to cross it, it would be better to ford it before this on good horses. Today five leagues.[167]

Tonight we observed the latitude and found ourselves at 41° 4'.[168] Figuring that we had not come up that much since Santa Mónica, and fearing some defect in the observation, we decided to make it by the sun the following day, halting at the hour best suited so as not to detain ourselves here where the Sabuaganas might disturb us.

164. The Colorado River. The expedition went from the campsite of Santa Rosalía up Jerry Gulch and across the top of Battlement Mesa at a point about 1/2 mile east of Castle Peak, then down Alkali Creek to a place where it reaches the plain on the south bank of the Colorado River. There the trail turns northward to the point of crossing. The party camped on the north bank of the Colorado River approximately 1 1/4 miles downstream from the present Una bridge.

165. On August 20 the expedition had decided to turn eastward from Dolores River to the land of the "Sabuagana Yutas," whom they later located on Grand Mesa. This is a vague reference to the headwaters of the Colorado River, one branch heading at Grand Lake just west of the Continental Divide in a segment of the Rocky Mountains lying north of the area where the Dolores and San Miguel rivers were said to head. See note 91 for earlier reference to Sabuagana Utes.

166. This must have been a temporary island in the river at that time.

167. Slightly over 13 miles.

168. Perhaps closer to 39° 30', though even this seems high, putting this sighting very near Rifle.

September 6

On the 6th we set out westward from the meadow and Río de San Rafael (where there are no prospects for a settlement). We went half a league downstream, another half through some narrow valleys to the west-northwest leaving the river to the south, to the northwest a quarter of a league, and through deep passes without rock for a league and a quarter west by west-northwest. We went west-northwest for about a mile and, after having gone nearly two more leagues westward over broken terrain with some stone and a lot of small pear cactus, went down to a little valley through which a small river of good water flows. At its edge, next to the only poplar that there is, and at eleven in the morning, we halted, ordering some companions to keep on going with the loose and loaded animals. The meridian was taken, and we found that we were at 41° 6′ 53″ latitude[169] and that there had been no error in last night's observation. We caught up with the other companions, who had stopped and were disgusted with the guide after having gone two leagues northwest; for, by leaving a trail which went upstream toward the west, and which seemed more direct according to reports, he was leading us along another one which enters a canyon and goes directly north—saying that the trail, even though it went northward through the canyon, made a turn to the west.

The companions conversant with the Yuta language tried to convince us that Silvestre the guide was leading us by that route either to keep us winding about so as not to proceed further or to hand us over to a Sabuagana ambuscade that could be awaiting us. To make the guide more suspect to us, they assured us of their having heard many Sabuaganas at the encampment telling him to lead us on the trail which went to the lake and, after having kept us needlessly winding around for eight or ten days, to make us turn back. And even though it was not altogether incredible that some could have said this, we never believed that the guide had agreed to it, nor even that it had actually happened, because not one of these companions of ours had told us anything like it up to here—the fact being that, while at the encampment, they did not cease magnifying other less fearsome difficulties, and more likely ones, and that in any ill event they risked only a bit less than we did.

169. Perhaps just slightly more than the observation of the previous night. They were at approximately 39° 33′.

We were well aware that in going north we were faced with a greater detour, but since Silvestre said that he led us up along that route because there was a bad upgrade on the other, we preferred to follow his judgment; but all the companions, except Don Joaquín Laín, argued hard for taking the other route, some because they overly feared the Comanches—and without foundation—and others because that route did not square with their own pet opinions, which were opposed to ours in no small degree. Then there arrived a Sabuagana Yuta, of the most northerly ones, and said that the north trail went up very farther on. As a result, we had to continue westward and, after going two leagues and crossing another rivulet, we halted by its edge, naming it La Contraguía.[170] Today seven leagues.[171]

Here were three camps of Sabuaganas, from which six men came over to our king's camp, among them one who had just come from the land of the Yamparica Comanches, where he had gone to steal horses with four others; and he said that the Comanches had gone farther away and that, from what the tracks showed, they were going to El Río de Napeste[172] or to the east. With this report our companions felt somewhat more at ease. These Sabuaganas were the last ones we saw.

September 7

On the 7th we set out from La Contraguía through a wide ravine in which, after going one league west, we found a meadow with very much pasturage. We turned northwest along the same ravine, and after going three leagues we paused awhile to let the horses drink, as we did not know if we would find water tonight. Afterward we kept on going in the same direction and, at a little more than a quarter league, swung north-northeast, going up an incline of so difficult an ascent that we doubted ever reaching the top because, besides its being very steep in places, there was not even a path and—as it consisted of very loose dirt—the mounts could not gain a sure foothold anywhere. Its ascent must be half a league long, and when one reaches the top there are some shelves of very brittle flagstone where two pack mules lost their footing and rolled down more than twenty yards at the least. But God

170. The campsite was near the confluence of Brush Creek with Roan Creek.
171. About 18.5 miles.
172. The Arkansas River.

willed that they did not tumble upon any of those following behind and that they came out unhurt.

We climbed it on foot with many exhausting and scary experiences. This is why we named it La Cuesta del Susto.[173] On it our guide gave us irrefutable proof of his sincerity and lack of guile. Having climbed the slope, we traveled half a league north-northeast, going down a short, narrow valley, and we stopped at a really scanty water spring, naming the site La Natividad de Nuestra Señora,[174] where there was middling pasturage for the mounts. Today a little more than five leagues and a quarter.[175]

September 8

On the 8th we set out from La Natividad de Nuestra Señora toward the north and went half a league, crossing an arroyo of good perennial water. Then, climbing up a steep incline, but without shelves and rock, we took a path—and better terrain than yesterday's—and, after going two and a half leagues northwest among spreading hills and some poplar groves, we reached a high ridge where the guide Silvestre pointed out to us the sierra on whose northern side dwell the Yamparica Comanches, who come to this one north of the Sabuaganas and to the point of the same sierra where his own people are—on the western side with respect to the spot from where he showed it to us.

We descended to the ridge down an extremely steep slope, rough in places but without rock, and with many clumps of scruboak and chokecherry which help prevent the mounts from slipping and rolling down. We entered an ample canyon of good terrain; then, after going a league north-northwest, counting the descent from the ridge, we turned north along it for a league and a half and halted so that the animals could drink—for a goodly amount of water which flows down from here, along the canyon route we took, either runs underground or dries up. In the afternoon we kept on going downstream through the canyon; after a league of travel west-northwest we stopped without water handy—because here the arroyo no longer has any—by a bend

173. "Shock (scare) Hill."
174. "The Nativity of Our Lady." Camp was situated on top of Brush Mountain, between Carr Creek and Brush Creek.
175. A little more than 13 3/4 miles.

with good pasturage, which we named Santa Delfina.[176] Today five leagues.[177]

September 9

On the 9th we left El Paraje de Santa Delfina along the same canyon, and having gone half a league northwest we swung north-northwest; then, after having trekked nine leagues in this direction all through the canyon over a well-beaten path—and with only one bad stretch, which can be avoided by crossing the stream a little ahead, and going across a thicket of high sagebrush and willows of the kind they call *latilla*[178]—we got out of it. Halfway in this canyon toward the south there is a quite lofty rock cliff on which we saw, crudely painted, three shields, or "Apache shields," of hide, and a spearhead. Farther down on the north side we saw another painting which supposedly represented two men in combat. For this reason we named it El Cañón Pintado,[179] and it is only through it that one can go from the ridge mentioned to the nearest river, for the rest of the terrain in between is very broken and rocky.

On this same side of the canyon, already near its exit, there is an exposed vein of metallic ore, but we were ignorant of its nature or quality, although one companion took one of the rocks fallen off the vein, and Don Bernardo Miera, showing it to us, said it was of the sort which miners call *tepustete*[180] and that it is an indication of gold ore. We neither decided nor shall we vouch for this, for not having mining expertise and because a more thorough testing is always required than what we could do at the time. Having passed the canyon, we traveled half a league north-northwest and came to a river which we named San Clemente;[181] we crossed it and halted on its northern edge, where there is a middle-sized meadow of good pasturage. This river is middling

176. Camp was located very near the junction of East Douglas and Cathedral creeks. The camp was about 2.5 miles beyond the junction of these creeks.

177. Thirteen miles today.

178. Genus *Helianthemum*.

179. "Painted Canyon," so called because of the Indian pictographs they saw. These pictographs are still there—located in Douglas Canyon south of Rangely, Colorado, and about half a mile above Philadelphia Creek and Big Bull Draw.

180. Perhaps iron pyrite, or "fool's gold."

181. The White River. Camp was located at the confluence of Douglas Creek and the White River at present Rangely, Colorado.

and flows west through here, and the terrain adjacent to it offers no prospects for a settlement. Today ten leagues.[182]

September 10

On the 10th—because, according to the interpreter, the guide kept saying that the next water source was too far away and that we could not reach it today even if we started early—we decided to cut the day's march in half; and so we set out after midday from El Río de San Clemente toward the northwest over rockless hills and brief plains with neither pasturage nor trees, and of very loose soil;[183] and traveled a league towards the west-northwest over rather level land and then another two leagues over dry arroyos and embankments. Then, because night was approaching and the terrain was not negotiable and perilous in the dark, we stopped in the box channel of an arroyo which we named El Barranco.[184] There was neither water nor pasturage in it, and so it became necessary to keep a watch over the animals and have them herded together all night. From the river up to here we traveled directly and without a path because, although there are several, they are those left by bison herds which come down to winter hereabouts. Today three leagues.[185]

September 11

On the 11th, as soon as it was full daylight, we set out from El Barranco and headed west-northwest; after going a league and a half through arroyos and embankments, some of them higher than yesterday's, we found in one of them a tiny spring of water from which the horses were unable to drink. We kept on going west-northwest for one league and climbed a ridge having an easy and not too high ascent. From it we traveled three leagues over good terrain with middling pastures. We caught sight of a poplar grove, and when we asked Silvestre if there was a water source there where he was leading us he said that there wasn't any, that it was an arroyo and not a river but that it might have water now. Thereupon we aimed for it and found plenty of running water for

182. Just over 26 miles.
183. They traveled over what is now the Rangely oil fields. Their description fits very closely the terrain of Raven Park.
184. "The Ravine." Probably on one of the dry arroyos near Stinking Water Wash. Perhaps this place itself. It provides the best level spot, with high walls which could help form a corral.
185. Slightly over 7 3/4 miles.

ourselves and for the horse herd, which was already much fatigued from thirst and hunger—and even a pack mule was so worn out that they had to remove the load it carried. In order to reach the arroyo we turned half a league north. Today six leagues.[186]

A short distance from El Barranco we had seen recent tracks of bison. We saw it again still fresher on the plain, and saw that it went in the direction we were taking. By now we had few provisions, in view of the long traveling we still had to do, because of what we had spent among the Sabuaganas and the other Yutas. And so, a little before reaching the arroyo, two companions took off and followed the tracks mentioned. A little after midday one of them returned saying that they had found the bison. We dispatched others on the fleetest horses and, after chasing it for about three leagues, they killed it; then at seven-thirty at night, they brought back a grand supply of meat (much more than what a big bull of the common variety has). And in order to prepare the meat so as to keep the heat from spoiling it for us, and at the same time to let the horse herd regain its strength; we spent the 12th at this place, which we named El Arroyo del Cíbolo,[187] without undertaking a day's march. Tonight it kept on raining for many hours.

September 13

On the 13th, about eleven in the morning, we set out from El Arroyo del Cíbolo over a plain lying at the foot of a small sierra which the Yutas and Lagunas call Sabuagari;[188] it extends from east to west, and its white cliffs can be seen from the high hills which come before El Cañon Pintado. After going west two leagues and three quarters, we arrived at the water source which the guide knew; it is a scanty spring and lies at the sierra's base almost at its western point. We continued for a quarter of a league in the same direction along a well-beaten path near which, toward the south, two copious springs of the finest water rise, a musket shot apart from each other, which we named Las Fuentes de Santa Clara.[189] The small plain over which they flow and are absorbed produces an abundance of good pasturage from their moisture

186. About 15 3/4 miles.
187. "Buffalo Arroyo." East of Snake John Reef and near the present K-Ranch. The expedition entered the present state of Utah at this point and followed Cliff Creek westward to the Green River Valley.
188. Probably the Sabuagana (today the Mowataviwatsiu). This is simply another spelling.
189. "The Fountains (Springs) of Saint Clair," located along Cliff Creek.

to which we descended and the horses consumed. From here we went a league northwest over the trail mentioned and crossed an arroyo which was coming down from the plain of Las Fuentes, and in which there were large waterholes. From here downstream there is a lot of good pasturage in its box channel bed, which is wide and level. We crossed it again, went up some low hills with finely ground rock in spots, and after going two leagues northwest came to a large river which we named San Buenaventura.[190] Today six leagues.[191]

This river is the most copious one we have come by, and the same one which Fray Alonso de Posada,[192] Custos of this [Custody] of New Mexico in the century gone by, relates in his report as separating the Yuta nation from the Comanche, according to the indications he gives in it and the distance at which he locates it with respect to Santa Fe. And in fact it is the boundary between these two nations, along the northeast and the north. Its course along here is to the west-southwest but, ahead and down to here, to the west. It comes together with the San Clemente, but we do not know if it does with the preceding ones. Here it has a meadow abounding in pasturage and good land for farming with the help of irrigation, which in width might be more than a league and in length could reach five. It flows into it between two lofty stone hogbacks which, after forming a sort of corral, come so closely together that one can barely make out the gorge through which the river comes.

According to our guide, one cannot cross anywhere else than by the single ford it has in this vicinity, which lies on the side west of the hogback on the north, very near to a chain of small bluffs of loose dirt,

190. The Green River. The Indians called it the "Seeds-Kee-dee." The camp was in a cottonwood grove some six miles north of present Jensen, Utah, on the east side of Green River, opposite the mouth of Brush Creek, which flows into the Green River from the west.

191. About 15 3/4 miles.

192. Fray Alonzo de Posada's report, written in 1686, was regarded for many years subsequent to that date as the most authentic source of information relating to the regions outside the settled portions of New Mexico, and particularly with respect to Quivira, Teguayo, and other distant provinces. Escalante had made careful studies of and had familiarized himself with many of the explorations which had been made into the territory which interested him so deeply. He had access to many documents relating to these explorations and discoveries, which, unfortunately, were destroyed during the Indian revolts in New Mexico, or have, during the years, disappeared for one reason or another. (See Auerbach, *Escalante's Journal*, p. 57.) See also S. Lyman Tyler, "The Report of Fray Alonso de Posada in Relation to Quivira and Teguayo," *New Mexico Historical Review* 33 (October 1958): 285–314.

some lead colored and others of a yellow, hue. It consist of finely
ground rock, and there the water does not reach the mounts' shoulder
blades, whereas everywhere else that we saw they cannot cross without
swimming. We halted by its southern edge about a mile from the ford;
we called the site La Vega de Santa Cruz.[193] The latitude was taken by
the North Star, and we found ourselves at 41° 19′ latitude.[194]

September 14

On the 14th we made no day's march, holding back here so that the
horse herd, which was quite weak by now, could regain its strength.
Before noon the quadrant[195] was set up to check the observation by the
sun, and we found no more than 40° 59′ 24″.[196] We concluded that this
discrepancy could perhaps result because the needle deviated here, and
to find this out we left the fixed quadrant set toward the north, along
the needle's meridian, until night time. As soon as the North, or polar,
Star was sighted, the quadrant being on the meridian mentioned, we
observed that the needle was swinging northeast. We again took the
latitude bearings by the North Star and came up with the same 41° 19′
of the previous night.[197]

At this place there are six big black poplars which have grown in
pairs attached to one another, and they are the ones closest to the
river. Near them is another one by itself; on its trunk, on the side fac-
ing northwest, Don Joaquín Laín dug out a small piece with an adze in
the shape of a rectangular window, and with a chisel carved on it the

193. "The Plain of the Holy Cross," on the Green River. See note 190 for the camp
location.
194. Their calculation was too high; they were at approximately 40° 24′.
195. This is the only mention of what type instrument they used in determining
their latitude positions. A quadrant measures angular altitudes. This instrument generally consists of a graduated arc of 90° or more, an index arm, and a sighting arrangement with a plumb line or spirit level. The quadrant was superseded by the sextant,
which determines geographic position by measuring the altitude of the sun and the
stars. They made their astronomical observations some fifteen times during the course
of the expedition. Seven times they fixed their position by the sun and eight times by
the North Star. It appears that most of their calculations were somewhat too high in
latitude. Just why this is so is not known. They were concerned about the accuracy of
their calculations and made several readings at the same place in order to check it more
accurately.
196. They recognized that their calculations were off and checked and rechecked
the latitude at night by the North Star and by the sun during the day. Their observations at night were more inaccurate than the ones during the day. Their campsite on
the Green River was at approximately 40° 24′.
197. Their calculations were about 55′ off—that is, too high.

inscription letters and numbers "Year of 1776," and lower down in a different hand "Laín" with two crosses at the sides, the larger one above the inscription and the other one beneath it.[198]

Here we were lucky to catch another bison smaller than the first one, although we enjoyed little meat because it had been overtaken late and very far from the king's camp. It happened also this morning that Joaquín the Laguna prankishly mounted an exceedingly spirited horse, and while racing over the meadow the horse stuck its forefeet in a hole and fell, discharging the horse-breaker a long distance off. We feared that the Laguna had been badly hurt by the thump; he, after having recovered from the surprise, was shedding a flood of tears. But God was pleased that all the damage was borne by the horse, which got its neck completely broken and was no longer useful.

September 15
On the 15th we made no day's march either, for the reasons given.

September 16
On the 16th we set out from La Vega de Santa Cruz (on El Río de San Buenaventura), went up about a mile to the north, arrived at the ford, and crossed the river. We took to the west and, after going one league along the northern side and meadow of the river, crossed another smaller one[199] which comes down from the northwest, and we entered it. Over the same meadow we turned south-southwest for a league and crossed another rivulet,[200] a little larger than the first, which comes down from the same northwesterly direction and enters the river. From both of them irrigation ditches could be dug for watering the land on this side, which is likewise good for farming even when they could not be conducted from the large river. We continued toward the southwest, getting away from the river, which swings to the south among hills and ravines of finely ground stone in spots. We descended to a dry arroyo

198. In 1950 Herbert E. Bolton (*Pageant in the Wilderness*, p. 170) claimed that "the six cottonwoods are still there, and are now huge trees." Botanists inform us, however, that the life of an average poplar (cottonwood) is only slightly more than one hundred years. Inasmuch as the tree was already a large one in 1776, it would seem unlikely that it would still be standing in 1950. Personnel from the University of Utah Botany Department, including Prof. Walter E. Cottam, cored all large cottonwood trees still standing at this site and found none of them to be more than seventy-five years old.
199. The Río de San Simón, or Brush Creek today.
200. Río de San Tadeo, now Ashley Creek.

down a long and very stony grade, its ascent on the other side being not as bad.[201]

As soon as we reached the top we found tracks of one or two days' imprint, of about twelve horses and some people on foot; and after a close study of the surroundings, indications were found that they had been lying in wait or spying for some time on the ridge's highest part, without letting go of the horses. We suspected that they might be some Sabuaganas who could have followed us to deprive us of the animal herd at this place, where we would likely attribute the deed to the Comanches instead of the Yutas, since we were no longer in the latters' country but the formers'.

What is more, Silvestre the guide gave us a strong basis for the suspicion the night before when casually and without being noticed he went off a short distance from the king's camp to sleep. All through the trip he had not worn the blanket we gave him, and today he left the place with it on, without taking it off all day, and we suspected that, for his having had an understanding with the Sabuaganas, he wore it so as to be recognized in case they attacked us. He increased our suspicion all the more when he lagged behind for a while, pensive and confused, before reaching the ridge where we found the tracks—now wanting to go along the river's edge, now to lead us along this route. We gave him no sign whatsoever of our suspicion by dissembling it altogether, but as our journey progressed he gave us convincing proofs of his innocence.

We continued exactly where the tracks led, descended once more to El Río de San Buenaventura, and saw that the ones making the tracks had stayed for a long while in the leafy poplar grove and meadow which it has. We kept on following it over the meadow by the river's edge, naming the site Las Llagas de Nuestro Padre San Francisco[202]—after having gone over the broken hills and slopes, and the meadow mentioned, six leagues to the southwest, and in the whole day's march eight leagues.[203]

As soon as we halted, two companions went southwest along the trail to explore the terrain roundabout and concluded that they had been Comanches.

201. Here they ascended to a pass through Asphalt Ridge. By a clumsy inversion, the padres describe the far side (the descent) and then compare it to the previous ascent.

202. Refers to the stigmata of Saint Francis. Means "The Wounds of Our Father Saint Francis." Located on the "Stirrup" bend of Green River.

203. About 21 miles.

✠

LAS LLAGAS–SAN ANDRÉS
SEPTEMBER 17–SEPTEMBER 26

September 17

On the 17th we set out from the meadow of Las Llagas de Nuestro Padre San Francisco toward the southwest, went up some low hills, and after going a league left the path we were following, the one on which the tracks of horses and people continued. Silvestre told us that they were Comanches who were going in pursuit of the Yutas who, while likely on a bison hunt, had made their presence felt. We convinced ourselves of this, from the direction they were taking as well as from other signs they left. We crossed a dry arroyo, climbed up a hill, and after going west a league and a half over good terrain, almost flat and arid, arrived at a high ridge[204] from which the guide pointed out to us the junction of the rivers San Clemente and San Buenaventura, which, now joined together,[205] flowed to the south with respect to where we stood.

We descended to a plain and another river's large meadow, and, after going west another league and a half, arrived at the juncture of two medium-sized rivers which come down from the sierra which lies near here and to the north of El Río de San Buenaventura. The one more to the east before the juncture runs to the southeast, and we named it Río de San Damián;[206] the other to the east, and we named it Río de San Cosme.[207] We continued upstream along the latter, and af-

---

204. At this point the guide, Silvestre, led them away from the Old Ute Trail, heading almost directly west across a shallow dry valley and west across the bench. Jutting out from this bench are many cliff edges providing overlooks over Ouray Park and Pelican Lake. Tucked back among them, and in many ways seemingly insignificant, is an unnamed mesa higher than all the rest. It lies in almost a direct line from Las Llagas to the confluence of the Uintah and Duchesne rivers and therefore is undoubtedly the "high ridge" from which Silvestre pointed out the joining river systems of the White (San Clemente) and the Green (San Buenaventura). This overlook knowledgeably led the expedition through the Uintah Basin.

205. The San Clemente (White River) and the San Buenaventura (Green River) join at Ouray, Utah.

206. The Uinta River.

207. The Duchesne River.

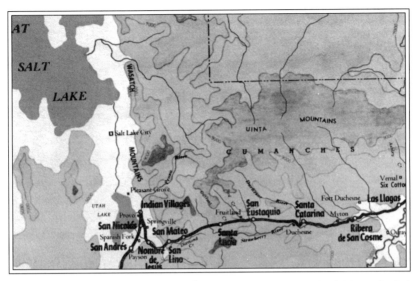

LAS LLAGAS TO SAN ANDRÉS, SEPTEMBER 17–SEPTEMBER 26

ter going west one league we saw ruins near it of a very ancient pueblo[208] where there were fragments of stones for grinding maize, of jars, and of pots of clay. The pueblo's shape was circular, as indicated by the ruins now almost completely in mounds. We turned southwest over a plain which lies between the two rivers, went up some hills of loose stone, and very troublesome to the already hoofsore mounts; we went down another meadow of El Río de San Cosme, and, having gone southwest for half a league and one-half toward the west over the meadow, we halted on it, naming it La Ribera de San Cosme. Today eight leagues.[209]

A little after we had stopped, we saw wisps of smoke at the sierra's base, and when we asked the guide who in his opinion had sent them up, he said that they could be Comanches or some of the Lagunas who usually came hunting hereabouts.

September 18
On the 18th we set out from La Ribera de San Cosme, and because the guide wanted to cross over to the river's other side and follow it, he stuck us through an almost impenetrable willow bosque, or thicket,

208. This site has not been identified by trail researchers.
209. Camp was just east of Myton, Utah. About 21 miles today.

and into marshy estuaries which made us backtrack and cross the river thrice while making many useless detours. Then over a plain next to its meadows we went three leagues west, turned west-southwest one league, crossed the river a fifth time, and again took to the west, in which direction we traveled three leagues and a quarter, now over the river's meadow, now over the plain next to it. We climbed up to a not very high mesa, flat on top and very stony, traveled for about three-quarters of a league, which includes the ascent and descent, crossed another small river which close to here flows into the San Cosme and which we named Santa Catarina de Sena,[210] and halted by its edge. Today nine leagues.[211]

From the encampment of the Sabuaganas and Paraje de San Antonino Mártir to here we tallied up eighty-eight leagues,[212] and from Santa Fe two hundred and eighty-seven.[213]

There is good land along these three rivers[214] that we crossed today, and plenty of it for farming with the aid of irrigation—beautiful poplar groves, fine pastures, timber and firewood not too far away, for three good settlements.

From the land of the Comanches a very long and high sierra comes down, running from northeast to southwest as far as the Lagunas, in what we could see for more than seventy leagues; at this season, toward the north from El Río de San Buenaventura, it displayed its tallest shoulders and peaks covered with snow, wherefore we named it Sierra Blanca de los Lagunas.[215] Tomorrow we shall begin climbing it and going across where it appears less lofty.

September 19

On the 19th we set out with no trail from El Río de Santa Catarina de Sena toward the southwest, went up a gradual and short but very rocky slope; then, after a quarter league we turned west, went down to El Río de San Cosme's edge, and traveled along it for two leagues and a quar-

210. The Duchesne River. They considered the present-day Strawberry to be the upper San Cosme or Duchesne River. The campsite was in a meadow on the western side of the Duchesne River and about a mile above the town of Duchesne, Utah.

211. A little more than 23.5 miles.

212. That is, 231.5 miles.

213. Over 750 miles from Santa Fe.

214. The three rivers mentioned are the lower Duchesne, the Lake Fork, and the upper Duchesne (named the Santa Catarina de Sena).

215. The Uinta Mountains.

ter, making several turns over almost impassable terrain, either because of so much rock or the rock-cliff precipices that are here. One of them caused one of our horses to be injured and made us backtrack about a mile and descend to another meadow of the river. We crossed it by breaking through a bosque of willow and tall bamboo reed and at half a league swung to the northwest by taking the channel bed of an arroyo for our route, ascending the sierra and leaving El Río de San Cosme behind.

We continued through the arroyo, which led us before we knew it into a canyon, narrow and tall on both sides with no other negotiable ground than the arroyo's channel bed. Halfway up the canyon there is another arroyo which comes from north to south. We continued northwest through the one we were following, and after going four leagues, which with the many windings came to be north-northwest, we got out of the canyon, which we named Las Golondrinas[216] for there being many nests of these birds in it, built with such symmetry that they looked like tiny pueblos. Then we continued over a sagebrush stretch of good terrain, and at half a league's travel west-northwest we swung west by going up a gradual hill with some tree growth; then, after descending it, we started over a plain across which a well-beaten path goes from north to south.

At the plain's end we descended by a high ridge, rocky and steep, to the water source which we named San Eustaquio,[217] having traveled two and a half leagues west. This water source is perennial and copious, and there is abundant pasturage by it. We arrived very tired, both on account of the day's march's painful travel and because a very cold west wind did not cease blowing very hard all day long. Today ten leagues.[218]

September 20

On the 20th we set out from San Eustaquio, leaving dead one of the strongest horses we had—it was the one which had broken its neck at

216. "The Swallows." In the bottomlands of Rabbit Gulch swallows are abundant, the reason given in the diary for the name *Las Golondrinas*. The trail crosses the highway to Tabiona about one mile north of its junction with U.S. 40.

217. Located in the meadows of Red Creek; however, the exact site of the camp cannot be identified, although a definite trail down from the ridge from the east somewhat fits the description. It is possibly two miles northwest from where U.S. Highway 40 crosses Red Creek.

218. About 25 1/3 miles.

Santa Cruz del Río de San Buenaventura. We went southwest up a long but gradual incline, then swung west for a little less than three leagues and a quarter over a stretch of sagebrush, flat but bothersome, and with a lot of small prickly pear cactus.

We entered a short, narrow valley, ample and gently sloping, and at a quarter league's travel south-southwest we turned west again and went down to a small river which runs east and could be the one we previously named San Cosme. We crossed the river, and to the west-southwest we went up another spreading incline, but gradual and easy to travel; then, after a mile we swung to the southwest for nearly two leagues through a very pretty and pleasant narrow valley with the most abundant pastures. We halted at the end of the narrow valley, at a small marsh with a good deal of pasturage, and which in the middle has a good water spring that we named Ojo de Santa Lucía.[219] Tonight it was so cold that even the water which stood close to the fire all night was frozen by morning. Today nine leagues.[220]

September 21

On the 21st we set out from El Ojo de Santa Lucía toward the southwest along the same narrow valley which we just ascended through a grove of white poplar, and after going a quarter league we swung west for a league and three-quarters, now over bothersome sagebrush stretches, now through low, narrow valleys of very soft dirt and many small holes in which, because they lay hidden in the undergrowth, the mounts kept sinking and stumbling at every instant. Then we went down to a medium-sized river[221] in which good trout breed in abundance, two of which Joaquín the Laguna killed with arrows and caught, and each one must have weighed more than two pounds. This river runs to the southeast along a very pleasant valley with good pasturages, many springs, and beautiful groves of not very tall or thick white poplars. In it there are all the conveniences required for a settlement. We named it Valle de la Purísima.[222]

219. At the top of Deep Creek drainage, one-half mile from Summit, alongside U.S. 40. From here the highway traveler passes along the Domínguez-Escalante trail west to the edge of Strawberry Reservoir.
220. Over 23.5 miles.
221. Trout Creek, now buried under the northeast bay of Strawberry Reservoir.
222. Strawberry Reservoir is now located here. From the present site of Duchesne, Utah, to present Strawberry Valley, the Domínguez-Escalante trail paralleled present U.S. Highway 40, keeping a mile or more to the north of it most of the way. That

The guide told us that in it for some time there had dwelt a portion of Lagunas, who depended on the said river's fishing for their more regular sustenance and who had moved out for fear of the Comanches, who were starting their incursions through this part of the sierra.

After crossing the river and climbing a hill, we came onto the valley floor; then, after going one league south-southwest through a narrow valley with a lot of sagebrush and bad surface, and at the end of three-quarters of a league, we crossed a small stream of very cold water.[223] We continued west another quarter league and entered a dense forest of white poplar, scruboak, chokecherry, and spruce; then, through the same forest we took the southern slope of a forested narrow valley, and after going a league west by south crossed over to the other side. The guide, anxious to get there sooner than we ourselves could make it, was hurrying so fast that he vanished in the forest at every step, and we knew not where to follow him because, what with the great density of the forest, there neither was a footpath nor could his track be discerned in many places. He was ordered to go slow and always within our sight.

We continued through the forest, which became denser the more we advanced, and after going west for half a league we emerged from it, arriving at a very lofty ridge.[224] From here the guide pointed out to us the side on which the lake lay, and to the southeast of it the other side of the sierra where he told us there lived a great number of people of the same language and type as the Lagunas. Along this ridge we went southwest for a quarter league and descended it, breaking through almost impenetrable swaths of chokecherry and scruboak and passing through another poplar forest so thick that we doubted if the packs could get through unless they were first taken off. In this forest the guide again began annoying us with his haste, so that we had to hold him back and never leave him to himself. In this dense growth Padre Fray Francisco Atanasio got a hard blow on one knee against a poplar tree.

We finally descended with great difficulty and labor into a deep and narrow valley in which, on finding enough of the pasturage which abounds throughout all this sierra, and water for ourselves and for the

portion of the trail leading from the ridge down to the east shore of Strawberry Reservoir is virtually that of the present highway.

223. Bryant's Fork, now covered by the waters of Strawberry Reservoir. Here they crossed a ridge dividing the Colorado River Basin from the Great Basin.

224. Strawberry Ridge at the top of Bryant's Fork.

animal herd, we halted in it after having traveled a league west in the descent, naming the site San Mateo.[225] Today six leagues and a half.[226] Tonight we felt the cold more than in the previous ones.

September 22

On the 22nd we set out from San Mateo to the southwest along this narrow valley's north slope,[227] on which there were many dangerous defiles and slides, with no other trail than the one we went opening all along, and over the sierra's corrugated ruggedness which all over here made us change direction and wind about excessively at every step; suffice it to say that, after going about five leagues up and down hills and lofty shoulders, some of them craggy with rock, we descended by a lengthy negotiable ridge-cut with many pastures onto a brief plain which lies between two rivulets that join each other on it, having traveled a league southwest along the cut. Our horses were much worn out, there was plenty of pasturage, and so we halted on it, naming it San Lino.[228] Today we traveled six long leagues[229] and, because of so much winding about, they must have amounted to three leagues toward the west-southwest with respect to San Mateo.

From the highest part of the last ridge-cut we saw a large number of big smoke signals being sent up, not too far away in the sierra itself and in front of us. Silvestre the guide said they belonged to some of his people possibly out hunting. We returned the message with others to avoid being mistaken, should they have seen us, for hostile people and so have them run away or welcome us with arrows. Again they began sending up bigger smoke clouds at the pass through which we had to go toward the lake—and this made us believe that they had already seen us, for this is the handiest and the regular signal used for anything worth knowing about by all the peoples in this part of America. Hence we reminded Silvestre to be on the lookout tonight in case one of his own, who knew of our arrival, approached the king's camp to find out what people were coming. And about two in the morning, the hour

225. On Sixth Water Creek, some two miles west of the summit.
226. About 17 miles.
227. They apparently crossed upper Diamond Creek and climbed around the north flank of Red Mountain, descending its western side.
228. Campsite was located at the junction of Wanrhodes Canyon and Diamond Creek—very near the present Palmyra Campground.
229. Because they made "long leagues" this date, they probably journeyed close to 16 miles.

when he figured we might have one or more close by, he spoke for a long while in their language, letting them know that we were peaceable folk, friendly and kind. We did not learn if anyone heard him.

September 23

On the 23rd, knowing that we were approaching the lake,[230] and so that both Silvestre and Joaquín would arrive in their country or homeland with greater joy and more affectionate toward us, we gave each one anew a yard of woolen stuff and another of scarlet ribbon, with which they promptly managed to trim themselves. Silvestre the guide donned the blanket he had gotten before as though it were a mantle or cape, and the woolen cloth we now gave him as a wide band around the head, letting the two long ends hang loose down the back. In this way he paraded about on horseback, the living image of the [ransomed] captives which the redemptive [Mercedarian] padres parade in their procession on this feast day of Nuestra Señora de la Merced.[231] This coincidence seemed like a happy omen of the good disposition of these captives, whose liberty we desired and besought of the Redeemer of the world through His immaculate Mother's intercession, who to encourage us to this end deigned to accept the title which the Church celebrates today.

We left San Lino early, heading southwest, went up a short hill, and on its top found a big anthill, all of very finely ground rock alum, cleaned and crystalline.[232] We went down the little Río de San Lino[233] and, after going a league along its brief meadows—which are very flat—without leaving the river, and alongside of it, we turned west downstream. Here another small one[234] enters it, and there are pretty bends in both of them and everything just right for sheepherding camps. After going west downstream for three-quarters of a league, we saw and passed by three copious springs of hot water that we touched

230. Utah Lake.

231. According to Msgr. Jerome Stoffel, September 23 was the Catholic feast day established in the Church calendar the previous century. It honored Mary, the Mother of Jesus Christ, as patron and consoler of those held captive. Hence the title Our Lady of Mercy. The padres saw it as an omen that they would enter the settlements of the Timpanogos people on this feast day in the Spanish concept of freeing these people from the slavery of sin and offering them the true freedom of Christ's redemption.

232. This hill has been identified by modern researchers. Evidence of "finely ground rock alum, cleaned and crystalline," is still in evidence.

233. Diamond Creek.

234. Upper Spanish Fork River.

and tasted, and it is of the same sulphurous quality as the one adjacent to El Pueblo de San Diego of the Jemez Indians in New Mexico.[235]

We continued west another three-quarters of a league, entered the narrowest part of the river's canyon,[236] and swung north for a mile. Here there are three other water springs like those immediately ahead, and all come out at the base of an extremely high mount very close to the river on this northern side, and they flow into the river. This is why we named it Río de Aguas Calientes.[237] In this narrow part of the canyon there are some difficult but improvable stretches.

We went for half a league northwest, crossed over to the other side of the river, went up a small hill,[238] and caught sight of the lake and spreading valley of Nuestra Señora de la Merced of the Timpanogotzis[239] (this is what we name it from here on). We also saw that they were sending up smoke signals on every side, one after another, thus spreading the news of our coming. We went down to the plain, already entering the valley; we crossed the river once more and, after going over its spreading meadows and along its northern edge for somewhat more than a league, we crossed to the other side and halted on one of its southerly meadows, which we named Vega del Dulcísimo Nombre de Jesús.[240] Today five leagues and a half.[241]

235. Castilla Hot Springs, once a favorite resort in Spanish Fork Canyon, just west of Thistle, Utah. Built in 1891, it was destroyed by fire in 1942.

236. Spanish Fork Canyon. The name "Spanish Fork" appears on John C. Fremont's map of the area published in 1845. Thus it was not, as local tradition has it, named by the early Mormon settlers of the region, who did not reach Utah until 1847. Mr. W. L. Rusho suggests that perhaps Fremont asked Kit Carson or Joseph Walker if the stream in question had a name and was told "Spanish Fork," named no doubt for the route taken to reach Utah Valley by the Taos trappers in 1824 and later. The route of the Domínguez-Escalante expedition was still virtually unknown in 1845, even though Baron Alexander von Humboldt had published a map of the area in 1811 based upon information he had acquired in the archives in Mexico. Fremont may have seen Humboldt's work and may have named it after the 1776 expedition, but we have no way of determining this with certainty.

237. Spanish Fork River.

238. Likely they climbed to the old lake bench at the mouth of Spanish Fork Canyon, from which they first viewed Utah Valley.

239. "Our Lady of Mercy of the Timpanogotzis." Utah Valley today.

240. "The Plain of the Most Sweet Name of Jesus." The campsite was located where the Spanish Fork River goes under present U.S. Highway 91 at its junction with U.S. Highway 50–6. It is on the main highway about two miles south of the town of Spanish Fork, Utah.

241. Almost 14.5 miles.

Through where we came we found the meadow's pastures recently burnt and other adjacent ones still burning. From this we inferred that these Indians had taken us for Comanches or other hostile people and, perhaps having seen that we brought horses, had tried to burn the pastures along our way so that the lack of them would make us leave the bottomland sooner. But since this is so large and extensive, they could not do it in such a short time, even though they had started fires in many places. This is why, while our small party stayed here, Padre Fray Francisco Atanasio set out for the first camps as soon as we halted, together with Silvestre the guide, his partner Joaquín, and Andrés Muñiz the interpreter. Then, after racing the horses as much as they could, even to the point of exhaustion, so as to get there this afternoon, and for six and a half leagues north-northwest, they got to them.[242]

Some men came out to meet them with weapons in hand to defend their homes and families, but as soon as Silvestre spoke to them the show of war was changed into the finest and fondest expressions of peace and affection. They very joyfully conducted them to their little humble abodes, and after he had embraced each single one and let them know that we came in peace, and that we loved them as our greatest friends, the padre allowed them time to talk at length with our guide Silvestre, who gave them an account so much in our favor of what he had observed and witnessed ever since he had become one of us, and about our purpose in coming, that we could not have wished for anything better.

He recounted to them at very great length how well we had treated him and how much we loved him. Then, among other things, he told them with greatest awe how, after the Sabuaganas had said that the Comanches would surely kill us or deprive us of our herds of horses, when we had passed through the places they frequent the most, and even found very fresh tracks of theirs, they had not attacked us nor had we seen them—what the padres had said thus coming true, that is to say, that God would deliver us from all our enemies and, as it came to pass in this manner, that even if we passed through their very own country they would not detect us nor we ourselves see them. He ended by saying that only the padres spoke the truth, that in their company

---

242. They traveled some 31.5 miles from San Lino to San Antonio—that is, from Wanrhodes Canyon in Diamond Fork Canyon to Dulcísimo Nombre de Jesús (Spanish Fork) and thence to the mouth of the Provo River on Utah Lake.

one could travel all over the earth without risk, and that they were nothing but good people.

They were further confirmed in this belief on seeing how the lad Joaquín was so haughtily proud of us that, paying little heed to his own, he would not leave the padre except to watch over the horses we brought along. Scarcely did he want to speak to them or in any way be near them, glued to the padre instead as he slept by his side through what was left of the night, which wasn't much—something truly a cause for amazement, not only on his people's part but on ours as well, for so remotely reared a child and Indian to so act who never outside of this period had seen either padres or Spaniards.

After they had spoken a long time about this, when many other individuals from adjacent camps had assembled, and he had given them all wherewith to smoke, the padre explained to them through the interpreter and Silvestre, who already had some grasp of it, the motives for our coming, and that the principal one was to seek the salvation of their souls and to show them the only means whereby they could attain it—the chief, primary, and necessary one being to believe in a single true God, to love Him and obey Him wholly by doing what is contained in His holy and spotless Law—and that all this would be taught them with greater clarity and at greater length, and the water of holy baptism poured on them, should they wish to become Christians and for the padres to come to instruct them and Spaniards to live among them, and that in this event they would be taught how to farm and raise livestock, whereby they would then have everything necessary in food and clothing, just like the Spaniards. For, by submitting themselves to live in the manner ordered by God and as the padres would teach them, our Great Chief whom we call King would send them everything that was needed, because, on seeing how they wished to be Christianized, He would already be regarding them as His children and would be caring about them as though they were already His people.

Afterward he told them that, since we had to continue our traveling in order to learn about the other padre, our brother, we needed another one from among their own to guide us as far as another nation they knew, which might grant us another guide. In all this Silvestre kept on helping us with his good offices. They listened gladly and replied that they were ready to do all this, revealing from the start their great docility. Although two chieftains had attended, but not the one who ruled over these people as the head one, the padre now asked these folk to send for him. They replied that his lodge was far away, but that he would come by morning. With this they retired to their lodges, some of them staying to converse all night with our Silvestre.

September 24

On the 24th we sent word by the interpreter mentioned, and by Joaquín and the other Laguna, for the companions to come from El Dulcísimo Nombre de Jesús to the Indian camp where we were and where the Indians from this and other encampments were steadily assembling, and they arrived here shortly before noon.[243] The head chief came early with the other two, several very old men, and many individuals. We laid before them at greater length what has already been told, and all unanimously replied that the padres should come, that they would live as the tatas (thus the Yutas call the friars) taught them, and that they offered all their land to the Spaniards for them to build their homes wherever they pleased—adding that they would scour the country and would always be on the lookout for entries made by the Comanches, so that when these tried to enter the valley and adjacent parts of the sierra they would be able to warn the Spaniards promptly and all joined together go out to punish them.

On seeing such a wonderful docility, and having achieved our purpose, we told them that at the end of our trip we would return with more padres and Spaniards and would baptize them and live among them, but that henceforth they should ponder well what they were saying lest they found themselves regretting it later on. They replied that they stood firm in what they were promising, adding most earnestly that we must not tarry long in returning. We told them that, even though all of our own people would believe whatever we apprised them concerning them, they should give us a token sign of their desire to become Christians[244] and so forth, in order for us to show it to our great chief and to the rest of the Spaniards, so that they would thereby

243. This entry is somewhat confusing. It appears that the day before only Domínguez, Andrés Muñiz, and the Indian guides proceeded to the campsite of San Antonio, at the mouth of the Provo River, on Utah Lake, leaving Escalante and the remaining members at Dulcísimo Nombre de Jesús. On the 24th the companions joined this group; yet the journal entry reads as if Father Escalante was already at San Antonio. At any rate, by noon of this date the party was all together once again near the mouth of present Provo River.

244. This token was later delivered to the governor of New Mexico by the padres.

be more readily convinced of their good desires and hasten their coming sooner. We did this to sound out their intentions more fully, and
they replied that they would most gladly and willingly furnish it the
next day in the morning.

Immediately we presented the chief, who had a genteel appearance,
with a big all-purpose knife and white glass beads, and Don Bernardo
Miera gave him a hatchet. To all the other individuals we gave white
beads, a few to each one since they were many, and for which they were
very happy and grateful. Afterward we reminded them of their promise
of a guide and told them that we would take Joaquín along with us if
they allowed it, for he wanted to continue with us. They replied that
they already had discussed the matter and that they had decided that
not only Joaquín but also the new guide, if he so wished, should go
along with us as far as our own country and that they could return with
us when we came back—adding that none of them knew much territory in the direction they knew we were about to take, but that with the
two, Joaquín and the guide, we could go on making inquiries among
the nations along our route. This so clear and satisfactory an expression of greatest sincerity filled us with unutterable joy, and it completely reassured us—the manner in which, without the least duplicity
and with spontaneous and free will, prompted by divine grace, they
accepted and desired Christianity.

We placed in front of them what we had given Silvestre, so that
when he saw it whosoever was to go with us as a guide might step
forth. Right away one of those standing about took it and now became
our guide and companion; him we dubbed José María from here on.
This done, we decided to resume our journey next day toward the establishments and port of Monterey.

They informed us that there was a sick child, for us to go over to
see him and baptize him. We went over, and, on finding him quite
grown up already and almost recovered by now from a long illness and
in no immediate danger, we did not see fit to pour the water of baptism
on him. Later on his mother brought him to where we were, begging us
to baptize him, but we comforted her instead by saying that we would
be coming back soon, when all, big and small, would be baptized.

At the very last, we let them know that we now had but few provisions and that we would be grateful if they sold us some dried fish.
They brought it and we bought a good portion. All day long and for
part of the night they kept coming to converse with us, and we found
them all very simple, docile, gentle, and affectionate. Already our Sil-

vestre was being looked up to with respect, and he was enjoying authority among them for his having brought us and because of our own regard for him.

September 25

On the 25th in the morning they assembled again and gave us the token requested, explaining to us what it contained. The day before, right after we had asked for it, we warned the interpreter that neither he nor the rest were to tell the Indians anything about this matter, so as to see what they of themselves would produce. But no sooner was the token sign presented than one companion—who knew nothing about the warning given—on seeing the figures on it, showed them the cross on the rosary and explained to them that they had to paint it on one of the figures. So then they took it back and painted a tiny cross upon each one. The rest of it stayed as it was, and they gave it to us saying that the figure which had the most red ochre along either side, or blood as they put it, represented the head chieftain because he had received the most wounds in battles with the Comanches; the other two, which were not as blood-smeared, the chieftains of lower rank than the first one; and the one which had no blood at all, one who was not a war captain but who wielded authority among them. These four male figures were crudely painted with earth pigments and red ochre on a short piece of tanned deerskin.

We accepted it, telling them that the great Chief of the Spaniards would be very much pleased when he saw it and that when we returned we would bring it with us so that they could see with what esteem we regarded their objects—and so that the painting itself would remind them of their promises and everything we had discussed. We told them that if, during the interval until we came, they suffered some hardship by way of illnesses or enemies they were to call upon God by saying, "God, the true One, help us, protect us." Then seeing how they could not pronounce these words correctly, we told them to say only, "Jesús-María, Jesús-María." This they began repeating with ease, our Silvestre very fervently excelling them in it, and during all the time we were making preparations to leave they did not cease repeating these holy names.

The hour arrived, and all bade us farewell most tenderly, especially Silvestre, who hugged us tightly, practically in tears. And they began charging us once more not to delay our return too long, saying that they expected us back within a year.

DESCRIPTION OF THE VALLEY AND THE LAKE OF NUESTRA
SEÑORA DE LA MERCED OF THE TIMPANOGOTZIS, OR
TIMPANOCUITZIS, OR COME PESCADO [FISH-EATERS].
THEY ARE CALLED BY ALL THESE NAMES.

Along the northern side of El Río de San Buenaventura, as we already
pointed out before, there is a sierra which extends from northeast to
southwest for more than seven leagues, from what we were able to see;
and it must be forty at the most in width or breadth and thirty where
we went across it. In this sierra toward the western side, and at 40° 49′
latitude[245] somewhat northwest by north of La Villa de Santa Fe, lies El
Valle de Nuestra Señora de la Merced of the Timpanocuitzis, surrounded by the sierra's heights from which four medium-sized rivers
that water it emerge, flowing through it until they enter the lake that it
has in the middle. From southwest to northeast the valley floor must
measure sixteen Spanish leagues (which are the ones we count in this
diary) and ten or twelve from northeast to southwest.[246] All of it is flat
and, with the exception of the marshes along the lake's edges, of very
good farmland quality for all kinds of crops.

Of the four rivers which water it, the first one toward the south is
the one of hot waters upon the spreading meadows, where there is sufficient irrigable land for two good settlements.[247] The second one,
flowing three leagues northward away from the first one and having
more water than it has, can sustain a good large settlement or two medium-sized ones, all with an abundance of irrigable lands. This one
splits into two branches ahead of the lake; on its banks are large alder
trees besides the poplars. We named it Río de San Nicolás.[248] Three
leagues and a half northwest from this one is the third, the area in between, consisting of flat meadows with good land for farming; it carries
more water than the foregoing two, has a larger poplar grove and
meadows of good soil which can be irrigated—all good for two or even
three good settlements. We stayed next to it through the 24th and 25th,
and named it Río de San Antonio de Padua.[249]

245. They were at the site of the present city of Provo, Utah, which is located at
40° 13′. They were off some 36′ in their calculation of the latitude at this point.
246. They calculated or estimated Utah Valley to be about 42 miles long and 26 to
32 miles wide. Their estimates are considerably too large.
247. On the Spanish Fork River.
248. Hobble Creek or Dry Creek.
249. The Provo River.

We did not get to the fourth river, although we made out its poplar grove. It lies northwest from that of San Antonio and has a great deal of level land extending in this direction, and good soil from what we saw. They told us that it carried as much water as the others, and hence some towns could be established on it. We named it Río de Santa Ana.[250] Besides these rivers, there are many small outlets of good water in the bottomland, and several small springs which come down from the sierra.

What we have finished saying concerning the settlements is to be understood as giving each one more land than it exactly needs. For if each town took only one league of farmland, as many Indian pueblos can fit inside the valley as there are those in New Mexico—because, even if along its upper reaches we give it the aforesaid measurements (which actually are greater), along the southern and other sides it has very ample nooks, and all consisting of good land. All over it there are good and very abundant pasturages, and in some sections it produces flax and hemp in such abundance that it seems as though it had been planted purposely. And the climate here is a good one, for after having experienced cold aplenty since we left El Río de San Buenaventura, we felt warm throughout the entire valley by day and by night.

Over and above these finest of advantages, it has plenty of firewood and timber in the adjacent sierra which surrounds it—many sheltered spots, waters, and pasturages, for raising cattle and sheep and horses. This applies along the north, the northeast, and the eastern and southeastern sides. Adjacent along the south and southwest it has two other extensive valleys, in the same manner abounding in pasturages and water sources. The lake reaches up to one of these, and after it a large, very nitrous, section of the valley follows. The lake must be six leagues wide and fifteen long;[251] it extends toward the northwest and, as we were informed, comes in contact through a narrow passage with another much larger one.

This one of the Timpanogotzis abounds in several species of good fish, geese, beavers, and other amphibious creatures which we did not have the opportunity to see. Round about it reside the Indians mentioned, who live on the lake's abundant fish, whence the Sabuagana

250. The American Fork River.

251. They calculated that Utah Lake was about 15 3/4 miles wide and about 39 1/2 miles long. It is actually about 13 miles wide at its widest point and about 25 miles long.

Yutas call them Fish-eaters. Besides this, they gather the seeds of wild plants in the bottoms and make a gruel from them, which they supplement with the game of jackrabbits, cottontail rabbits, and fowl, of which there is great abundance here. They also have bison handy not too far away to the north-northwest, but fear of the Comanches prevents them from hunting them.

Their dwellings are some sheds or little wattle huts of willow, out of which they have interestingly crafted baskets and other utensils for ordinary use. They are very poor as regards dress. The most becoming one they wear is a deerskin jacket and long leggings of the same. For cold seasons they wear blankets made of jackrabbit and cottontail rabbit furs. They employ the Yuta language but with noticeable variances in pronunciation, and even in some words. They possess good features, and most of them are fully bearded. All the sections of this sierra along the southeast, south-southwest, and west are inhabited by a great number of peoples of the same nation, language, and easy-going character as these Lagunas, with whom a very populous and extensive province could be formed.

In their language, the proper names of the chieftains contained in the painted token previously described are: Turunianchi for the head chief, Cuitzapununchi for the second one, and for the third one—who is our Silvestre—Panchucunquibiran (which means Great Talker); for the fourth one, who is not a chieftain and is the head chief's brother, Picuchi.

The other lake[252] with which this one comes in contact covers many leagues, so we were informed, and its waters are harmful and extremely salty, for the Timpanois assured us that anyone who wet some part of the body with them immediately felt a lot of itching in the part moistened. They told us that all around it there lives a numerous and secluded nation calling itself Puaguampe, which in our common speech means "bewitchers"; it employs the Comanche language, lives on wild plants, drinks from various springs or outlets of good water encircling the lake, and they have their small dwellings made of grass and sods—which must be the roofs of them. They are not foes of the Lagunas, as these gave us to understand, but ever since a certain incident when they came near and killed one of their men they do not consider them as neutral as before. On this occasion they came in through

252. Great Salt Lake, which is connected to Utah Lake by the forty-mile-long Jordan River.

the end of the gap of La Sierra Blanca de los Timpanois[253] (which is the same one where they reside), to the north by northwest from where these are. And right through here they say the Comanches make their sallies, which do not seem to be too frequent.

The Timpanogotzis are so named after the lake where they reside, which they call Timpanogó, and this name is the proper one for this lake since the name or word by which they designate any lake is *pagariri*. This one must be six leagues wide and fifteen long up to the narrow gap and its contact with the other, larger one.

September 25

On the 25th, about one in the afternoon, we left the first camps mentioned and Río de San Antonio by the same way we had come, and, after going a little more than three leagues and a half,[254] we stopped to spend the night at the edge of El Río de San Nicolás.[255]

September 26

On the 26th we left El Río de San Nicolás with the two Lagunas, José María and Joaquín, arrived at the Aguas Calientes, crossed it, and, after going two leagues south from the latter, halted while still on bottomland and close to an arroyo of good water, which we named Arroyo de San Andrés.[256] It seems to have constant flow and so is more correctly a small river or running spring than an arroyo. Along its edges there is a species of medium-sized to large-sized trees which breed on their foliage a great number of certain tiny living mites as foreign to our ken as they [the trees] are. Today two leagues.[257]

---

253. Mount Timpanogos (11,750 feet high). In late September it was probably covered with snow and thus gave rise to its name to the Spaniards of the "White Mountain of the Timpanogos Indians."

254. About nine miles.

255. The campsite was located on what is now called Dry Creek (formerly Hobble Creek) at this point. It is just east of Interstate 15 where Dry Creek passes under the freeway. This is just north and west of the present city of Springville, Utah.

256. Peeteetneet Creek. The campsite was located where the Payson Memorial Park now stands along Peeteetneet Creek.

257. They err on the total distance traveled this date. From the Río de San Nicolás (Dry Creek) to the Río de Aguas Calientes (Spanish Fork) is approximately two leagues (5.26 miles). From here to the Arroyo de San Andres (Peeteetneet Creek) is another two leagues (5.26 miles). The total distance traveled this date was four leagues, or about 10.5 miles. Not reckoning with this discrepancy has thrown trail researchers off since the time of Bolton's translation in *Pageant in the Wilderness* (1950).

✠

SAN ANDRÉS–SAN ELEUTERIO
SEPTEMBER 27–OCTOBER 10

September 27

On the 27th we started out from El Arroyo de San Andrés toward the south and, after going one league while still on bottomland, crossed another rivulet²⁵⁸ with as much water as that of a medium-sized irrigation ditch, and wherever it goes it follows the lay of the land, which is very good for farming. We continued south over the same bottomland for a league and a half, went through its southern pass—which we named Puerto de San Pedro²⁵⁹—and entered another spreading valley which, because the salt flats from which the Timpanois provide themselves lie very close to it on the east, we named Valle de las Salinas.²⁶⁰ This is one of those just mentioned above, and it must extend fourteen leagues from north to south and five from east to west. It is all level land, greatly abounding in water and pasturage, even though no river flows through it other than a small one. There a great number of fowl breed, the kind which we already spoke of in this diary. We went another four leagues south over the valley floor and stopped by a copious running spring of good water, which we named Ojo de San Pablo.²⁶¹

As soon as we halted, José María and Joaquín brought five Indians from the adjacent camps. We gave them something to eat and to smoke and proposed to them what we had to the others at the lake as circumstances warranted. We found them as docile and agreeable as the rest, displaying great joy on hearing that more padres were to come and the

---

258. The line of travel took the party near the present route of U.S. Highways 50, 6, and 91, in a southwesterly direction. The rivulet which they crossed is now called Spring Creek.
259. "St. Peter's Gates." This marks the dividing line between Utah and Juab counties. It is a gentle pass, through which the new Interstate 15 passes.
260. Now called Juab Valley, Utah.
261. These "copious springs" are now known as Burriston Ponds and are located approximately 1.3 miles south-southwest of the town of Mona, Utah.

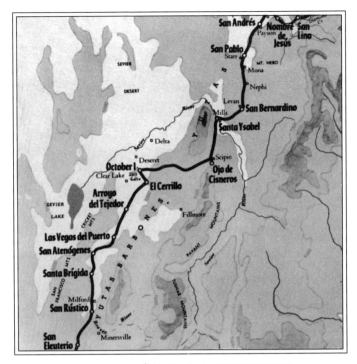

SAN ANDRÉS TO SAN ELEUTERIO
SEPTEMBER 27–OCTOBER 10

Spaniards to live among them. They stayed with us until almost midnight. Today six leagues and a half[262] to the south.

September 28

On the 28th we set out from El Ojo de San Pablo, headed south, and, after going four leagues, arrived at a small river[263] which comes down from the eastern side (with respect to the river) of the sierra where the salt flats are, according to what they told us. We tarried here a short while in the shade of the poplars on its banks to get some relief from the prevailing great heat, and scarcely had we sat down when from among certain thick clumps of willows eight Indians approached us with great fear, most of them naked with only a piece of buckskin over the private parts. We spoke to them and they to us, but without un-

262. Very close to 17 miles.
263. Four Mile Creek today. This stream is pictured on the Miera map.

derstanding one another, for the two Lagunas and the interpreter had gone on ahead. We made them understand by signs that we were people friendly to them and came in peace. We continued south and, after going three leagues, turned southeast for half a one; another half to the south, we stopped while still in the valley near a spring which we named San Bernardino.[264] Today eight leagues,[265] all almost south.

September 29

On the 29th we left San Bernardino, heading south-southwest. Then we met six Indians, talked a long while with them, and preached to them through the interpreter and the Lagunas while they listened with great docility. After going two leagues and a half we turned southwest, already leaving El Valle de las Salinas,[266] which still continues south. Here we came upon a very old Indian of venerable countenance. He was alone in a tiny hut, and he had a beard so full and long that he looked like one of the ancient hermits of Europe. He informed us about an adjacent river and about some of the country which we still had to travel. We went southwest for half a league, swung more to the west-northwest through some little ravines and arid hills,[267] and, after going a league and a half, reached the river without seeing it until we were at its very edge,[268] and halted on a short meadow of good pasturage, which we named Santa Isabel. Here we took latitude bearings by the North Star and found ourselves at 39° 4' latitude.[269]

Shortly after we halted, four Indians arrived on the other side. We had them cross over to where we were and made them feel at home, and they stayed with us all afternoon. They informed us of the terrain

264. These springs are located in a pasture about 4.2 miles southwest of Levan, Utah, just off U.S. Highway 91. This campsite had water, but that is about all.
265. Twenty-one miles.
266. The party left present Juab Valley in a west-southwesterly direction on the route of what is now Old Botham Road.
267. Through Washboard Valley.
268. It is easy to see how they could not see the river until they stumbled upon it. The valley is extremely flat and covered with sagebrush, and at this point the river has carved a narrow channel, which is somewhat below the level of the sagebrush. The river suddenly looms up in front of you. The Río de Santa Isabel is now known as the Sevier River.
269. Campsite was on the Sevier River near the point at which U.S. Highway 91 crosses the river. The valley at this point is called today Mills Valley. The latitude here is 39° 13', not 39° 4' as recorded.

they knew and of the water source to which we should go the following day.

This river, according to the name these Indians have for it, appears to be the San Buenaventura, but we doubt that this can be so since here it carries much less water than where we crossed it at 41° 19' (see the entries for September 13 and 14)—the fact being that after it joins the San Clemente, the San Cosme and San Damián enter it along with other rivulets. Moreover, it seems likely that when we crossed it, at said latitude, Silvestre would have told us that this river ran near his country, as he told us other things about the sierra, other rivers, and the lake, which data we brought along according to his information, in which the one he included is this one passing through Santa Isabel.

September 30

On the 30th, very early, twenty Indians arrived in the king's camp along with those who came yesterday afternoon, all covered with blankets of cottontail and jackrabbit furs. They stayed talking very happily with us until nine in the morning, as docile and agreeable as those before. Now these ones, more fully bearded than the Lagunas, have their nostril-cartilage pierced, and in the hole, by way of adornment, they wear a tiny polished bone of deer, fowl, or some other animal. In their features they more resemble the Spaniards than they do all the other Indians known in America up to now, from whom they differ in what has been said. They employ the same language as the Timpanogotzis. From the river and site of Santa Isabel onward begin these full-bearded Indians, who perhaps gave rise to the report about the Spaniards who were said to exist on the other side of El Río del Tizón;[270] this, according to several collated reports, is El Río Grande, which is formed from the Dolores and others and joins the Navajo.

At nine we left Santa Isabel, crossed the river, and traveled south for three leagues and a half over a plain thick with sagebrush which harassed the horses. We went into a small canyon with good terrain, and at a short distance onto a plain abounding in pasturage but waterless; then, after traveling south on it for a league and a half, we found behind some low hills a good water spring, which we named El

270. The persistent legend, fostered by the Indians, of bearded men living north of the Colorado River, supported the equally persistent speculation of a colony of shipwrecked Spanish sailors far to the north. Escalante, in his previous reports, had already expressed his own disbelief regarding this legend.

Ojo de Cisneros.[271] By it there are two small trees which reveal its location. Today five leagues[272] south.

October 1

On the 1st of October we left El Ojo de Cisneros, going back nearly half a league toward the north. We again took to the south and, after going a quarter league through a narrow valley[273] which was rocky in places, climbing in it a ridge-cut of the sierra (since El Valle de las Salinas continues to the south), we swung southwest for a quarter league and discovered a most spacious plain surrounded by mountains in which they had told us El Río de Santa Isabel entered another lake, and leaving it again continued toward the west.[274]

Having descended the ravine, or pass, we took to the west-northwest over low hills with a great deal of rock and, having gone two leagues, we entered a sagebrush stretch and traveled three leagues west along the edge of a dry arroyo[275] without a trail. We left the arroyo and, after going two leagues west by north, turned toward the plain. We thought we saw marshland or lake water nearby, hurried our pace, and discovered that what we had judged to be water was salt in some places, saltpeter in others, and in others dried alkaline sediment. We kept on going west by south over a plain and salt flats and, after traveling more than six leagues, we halted without having found water fit to drink or pasturage for the horses, since these already could go no farther. There was some pasturage where we stopped, but bad and scarce. All over the plain behind there had been none, either good or bad. Today fourteen leagues.[276]

Two companions had gone ahead in search of water, and they said

271. The campsite was located about 2.5 miles southwest of the town of Scipio, Utah, in a depression formed by the Pahvant Mountains. It was near the edge of the present Fishlake National Forest.

272. Thirteen miles.

273. Through Scipio Pass, through which U.S. Highway 91 and Interstate 15 travel.

274. Curiously they did not pursue this possibility of a water route west, possibly because the Indians knew of no peoples in that direction, but also because they were soon to experience the lack of water and forage.

275. Eight Mile Creek.

276. They traveled over 36 miles on this date. The campsite of October 1, which the padres called Llano Salado ("Salt Plain"), doubtless in an attempt to reflect the desolate nature of the area and their own discouragement due to lack of fresh water and pasturage, was located on the edge of salt marshes about 4.5 miles northwest of Pahvant Butte, in Juab County.

that they had seen some a league farther on beyond this place. Upon this report we decided that as soon as the moon came up they would take the horse herds at a slow pace to have them drink, and bring back water for the men. They did not come upon the water previously seen, and so, leaving two behind with the horse herd, the other three went off to look for it in the direction where, they had told us, El Río de Santa Isabel was with respect to our position.

October 2

On the 2nd of October morning came without our knowing anything about the five who had gone looking for water, nor about the horse herd. One of the two who had stayed with the latter came at six in the morning unable to account for it, or his companion or the others, because these two had fallen asleep. The horse herd had wandered off, driven by thirst, and they had awakened in turn, each one taking a different direction to look for it. Right away Don Juan Pedro Cisneros rode off bareback following the track and overtook it [the herd] seven leagues to the rear, that is, halfway on the preceding day's route, and returned with it almost at midday. A little later those who had gone in search of water arrived with some Indians, into whose camps they had stumbled, these being located at the edge of El Río de Santa Isabel.

These were from among the full-bearded and pierced-nose ones, who called themselves Tirangapui[277] in their language. The five of them who came first with their chief were so fully bearded that they looked like Capuchin padres or Bethlehemites.[278] The chief was already advanced in years, yet not aged, and of very good appearance. They stayed talking very happily with us, and in the briefest time won our great affection.

The chief learned that one of our companions was still missing; promptly he ordered his four Indians to lose no time in looking for him on the plain and to bring him back to where we were, each one taking a different direction. It was a gesture deserving the greatest gratitude and worthy of admiration in so wild a folk who had never before seen people like us. While busy giving these orders, the chief saw the one who was missing already returning and very joyfully apprised

277. These "Bearded Utes" were probably Southern Paiutes.

278. Refers to the fact that friars in some religious orders were accustomed to wearing long beards.

us of it. We announced the Gospel to them as well as the interpreter could manage it, explaining to them God's oneness, the punishment He reserves for the wicked, the reward He gives to the righteous, and the necessity of holy baptism and of the knowledge and observance of the divine law.

While this was going on, three others of them were seen coming toward us, and then the chief told us that they also belonged to his people, and for us to hold up the conversation until they arrived so that they too could hear everything we were telling them for their benefit; then, when they arrived, he told them that we were padres and that we were instructing them in what they had to do in order to go to heaven, and so to be attentive. He told them this so efficiently that, while we understood only one or the other term in Yuta, we gathered what he was telling them before the interpreter gave it to us in translation, merely by the gestures with which he expressed himself. We told them that if they wanted to attain the blessings proposed we would come back with more padres so that all could be instructed, as would those of the lake who were awaiting the friars, but that in such an event they were not to live scattered about as now but gathered together in towns.

They all replied very joyfully that we must come back with the other padres, that they would do whatsoever we taught them and ordered them to do—the chief adding that then, if we so wished and deemed it more advantageous, they would go to live with the Lagunas (which we likewise had proposed to them). We took our leave of them, and all, the chief especially, kept holding us by the hand with great tenderness and affection. But where they expressed themselves the most was when we were already leaving this place. Scarcely did they see us depart when all—following their chief, who started first—burst out crying copious tears, so that even when we were quite a distance away we kept hearing the tender laments of these unfortunate little sheep of Christ, lost along the way simply for not having the Light. They touched our hearts so much that some of our companions could not hold back the tears.

At this site, which we named Llano Salado—where, because of some white and thin shells that we found, there seems to have been a lake very much larger than the present one—we observed the latitude, which was 39° 34′ 36″.[279] This observation was made by the sun almost

279. Somewhat too high in their calculations. It is closer to 39° or slightly less.

at the middle of the plain, which from north to south must be a little less than thirty leagues and from east to west fourteen. It is very sparse in pasturages in most places; and though two rivers run into it, the Santa Isabel from the north and the other medium-sized one from the east, the waters of which are very brackish, we did not see any location suitable for settlement.

In the afternoon we pursued our journey to the south-southeast because the marshes and lakes were not letting us go south, which was the direct route to the pass through which we were to leave the plain. After going three leagues we halted near a small bluff which stands on it. Wherefore we named the stopping point, where there were marshes with much pasturage but with brackish water, El Cerrillo.[280] Today three leagues.[281]

October 3

On the 3rd we left El Cerrillo, made several detours because we were surrounded by marshes,[282] and decided to cut across by going over the east river mentioned, which appears to sink into them and the plain's other lakes—and which abounds in fish. The ford was sticky and miry, and in it the mount which Andrés the interpreter was riding fell and pitched him into the water, dealing him a hard blow on one cheek. The crossing having been made with some labor, after we had gone six leagues south by west over flat and good terrain we came to an arroyo which seemed to have much water, but we found only some waterholes where the horse herd might be able to drink with difficulty. Nevertheless, we stopped here because there was good pasturage. All over the arroyo there was a kind of white scum, dry and thin, which looked from afar like linen spread out, for which reason we named it Arroyo de Tejedor.[283] Today six leagues[284] south by west.

October 4

On the 4th we set out from El Tejedor up the arroyo toward the south, and at the quarter league swung a little to the south-southwest; then,

280. Near Pahvant Butte. Clear Lake Waterfowl Refuge is located nearby.
281. Very close to eight miles.
282. Around Clear Lake where the present state waterfowl refuge is located.
283. Beaver River. They called it Arroyo of the Weaver because it appeared to have linen spread out to dry along its banks. The campsite was located where the desert road from Clear Creek reaches the Beaver River, about four miles south of where the river passes under the Union Pacific Railroad tracks and Utah State Highway 257.
284. About 15.5 miles.

after going somewhat less than five leagues, we reached the south pass and exit of Llano Salado.[285] In the arroyo mentioned we found more water, not as bad as yesterday's, and beautiful meadows greatly abounding in good pasturage for the horse herds, which by now were very much exhausted because the brackish waters had done them much harm. And so we stopped here, naming the site Las Vegas del Puerto.[286] Today five leagues.[287]

October 5

On the 5th we set out from Las Vegas del Puerto, heading south along the same arroyo's edge, and after going two leagues we turned southwest for three leagues and halted in another meadow of the arroyo, naming it San Atenógenes.[288] Today five leagues.

This morning, before we left Las Vegas del Puerto, José María the Laguna turned back and left us without an adieu. We saw him leave the king's camp but did not want to say anything to him, nor to have him followed and brought back, so as to allow him complete liberty. We did not know what moved him to this desertion, although, according to what the interpreter told us afterward, he already came somewhat disconsolate on seeing that we were getting so much farther away from his country. But undoubtedly an unexpected incident of the night before brought it to a head. This happened when, after Don Juan Pedro Cisneros had summoned his servant Simón Lucero to pray the Virgin's rosary with him and with the others and the latter refused to come, he reprimanded him; and as he was scolding him for his laziness and lack of piety, the servant took him on, grappling with him arm to arm.

Had we not, as soon as we heard the disturbance from where we were in the act of anticipating the Morning Hours of prayer, gone on to finish them—but not soon enough—it would not have frightened the said José María so much. We tried to convince him that those involved were not angry at each other, and that even when a parent corrected his youngster as it now had happened, they never reached the point of kill-

285. This "South Pass" separates Black Rock Desert from the Escalante Desert. It marks the exit from the Llano Salado (Salt Plain) into Beaver Bottoms, which forms the northern reaches of the Escalante Desert.
286. Located about 7.5 miles south of Bloom Siding on the Union Pacific Railroad line and west of the Beaver River.
287. Thirteen miles.
288. Located approximately 2.5 miles west-southwest of Black Rock Siding on the Union Pacific Railroad line and just northeast of Red Rock Knoll.

ing each other as he was thinking, and therefore that he should not be scared. Nevertheless, he turned back from here, while we were left without anyone who knew about the country ahead, even if from hearsay. We felt very bad about this incident because we had wanted to hasten his salvation, which now he will not be able to attain that soon.

After we halted, two went off to find out if the sierra's western side, and likewise the valley that was there, could be negotiated and furnished any hope of finding water sources and pasturages for the horse herds. It was already dark when they returned saying that they had not found any pass for traversing the sierra, that it was very high and rugged from this direction, and that ahead of it lay a wide plain without any pasturage or water source whatsoever. This being so, we could no longer take this direction—which was the best for getting to Monterey, where our goal lay—and we decided to continue south until we crossed the sierra mentioned through a very wide valley which begins at this Paraje de San Atenógenes and which we named Valle de Nuestra Señora de la Luz.[289] Through it El Arroyo del Tejedor continues with sufficient waterholes or banked ponds of good water and very spacious meadows abounding in pasturage, of which this valley is very scarce.

On the two preceding days a very cold wind from the south had blown fiercely without ceasing. This brought on a snowfall so heavy that not only the sierra's heights but even all the plains were covered with snow tonight.

October 6

On the 6th, morning came with snow falling, and this went on all day long without ceasing, and for this reason we could not undertake a day's march. Night came and, on seeing that it would not stop, we implored the intercession of Our Mother and Patroness by praying aloud in common the three parts of her rosary and by chanting the Litany, the one of All-Saints. And God was pleased that by nine at night it should cease to snow, hail, and rain.

October 7

On the 7th we could not depart from San Atenógenes either, although we were in great distress, without firewood and extremely cold, for with so much snow and water the ground, which was soft here, was unfit for travel.

289. "The Valley of Our Lady of the Light." In the Beaver River Bottoms.

October 8

On the 8th we set out from San Atenógenes over the plain toward the south. We traveled only three leagues and a half with great difficulty, because it was so soft and miry everywhere that many pack animals and mounts, and even those that were loose, either fell down or became stuck altogether. We stopped about a mile west of the arroyo, naming the place Santa Brígida,[290] where, after having taken a bearing by the North Star, we computed 38° 3' 30" of latitude. Today three leagues and a half[291] to the south.

Today we suffered greatly from the cold because the north wind did not cease blowing all day, and most acutely. Up to here we had kept our intent of reaching the garrison and new establishments of Monterey. But, figuring that we were still distant from them, although we yet had to descend only one degree and 23 1/2 seconds to this Paraje de Santa Brígida, we had advanced westward only 136 1/2 leagues, according to each day's directions. And as for the conclusion we were making, partly from not having found among all these latter peoples any reports about the Spaniards and padres of the said Monterey, partly because of the great difference in longitude with which this port and La Villa de Santa Fe are shown on the maps, we had many leagues left to us toward the west.

Since winter had already set in most severely, for all the sierras we managed to see in all directions were covered with snow, the weather very unsettled, we therefore feared that long before we got there the passes would be closed to us, so that they would force us to stay two or three months in some sierra where there might not be any people or the wherewithal for our necessary sustenance. For the provisions we had were very low by now, and so we could expose ourselves to perishing from hunger if not from the cold. We also figured that, even granting that we arrived in Monterey this winter, we could not be in La Villa de Santa Fe until the month of June the following year.

This delay, along with others which will arise during the ordinary and necessary pursuit of so interesting an undertaking as the one we have been treating, could be very prejudicial to the souls which, as mentioned before, yearn for their eternal salvation through holy bap-

290. Located about 11.5 miles south-southwest of Black Rock Siding and 11 miles due north of the town of Milford, Utah. The latitude reading 38° 3' 30" is too low. They were slightly higher at 38° 33'.

291. About 9 miles.

tism. These, on seeing such a great delay in what we promised, would feel frustrated in their hopes, or they would conclude that we had purposely deceived them. As a result, their conversion and the extension of his majesty's dominions in this direction would become much more difficult in the future. To this could be added the possibility that Joaquín the Laguna, frightened and vexed by so many hardships and want, could wander off or return to his country or to other peoples he might have heard about, as did the other one.

Weighing all this, therefore, and that by continuing south from Santa Brígida we could discover a shorter and better route than that of the Sabuaganas to go from Santa Fe to La Laguna de los Timpanois and to these other full-bearded Indians—and perhaps some other nation heretofore unknown which may always have been living in the region north of El Río Grande—we thereupon decided to continue south for as much as the terrain permitted as far as El Río Colorado, and from here point our way toward Cosnina, Moqui, and Zuni.[292]

NEW ITINERARY AND START OF OUR RETURN FROM 38 DEGREES, 3 MINUTES, 30 SECONDS LATITUDE

October 9

On the 9th we set out from Santa Brígida, headed south, and, after going six leagues with less trouble than yesterday, for the ground being less soft and no longer as wet, we stopped near a nook formed by the valley and great plain of Nuestra Señora de la Luz, from where it continues wider and for many leagues to the southwest. We named the stopping point San Rústico.[293] Here, for our not having to go near the arroyo for water or near its meadows for pasturage, we found it all very convenient. The water was from the rains and not permanent. Today six leagues[294] south.

October 10

On the 10th we left San Rústico, headed south, went one league, and, after going three more leagues south-southwest, came to a short and

292. They had in mind, apparently from the beginning of the expedition, to return by way of the Cosnina (Havasupai) Indians, testing the trail which had been described by Escalante in the summer of 1775 and which Father Garcés had traveled in the spring and summer of 1776.

293. Located some 6.5 miles south of the Milford railroad station on the southward extension of Utah State Highway 129. It is still somewhat west of the Beaver River.

294. About 15.6 miles.

very low hill standing in the middle of the plain; so as to survey by eye the extent of this valley and plain of La Luz, we climbed the hill and saw that from here toward the southwest it stretched for more than thirty-five or forty leagues, for where it ends in this direction one could barely discern the sierras, these being very high, as we saw better later on. We also saw three outlets of hot sulphurous water which are on the top and the east flank of said hill.[295] Around it below are other short patches of nitrous soil. We continued over the plain and, after going two leagues south, we halted, fearing that farther on we would not find water for tonight. Here there was a large good quantity of it from the melted snow, dammed up like a lake; there was also good pasturage. We named the site San Eleuterio.[296] Today six leagues.[297]

The full-bearded Yutas extended this far south, and here their territory ends apparently.

295. The hill with the hot springs on its east side and top is the northernmost of two low hills lying south of Thermo Siding on the Union Pacific Railroad line. The water today is warm to hot, and sulphurous. This is an important reference point in determining distances because the hill is a landmark which can be pinpointed with considerable certainty.

296. Brown Knoll, about two miles east of the Union Pacific Railroad tracks. There is a small ravine in the eastern ridge of the knoll which would have been ideal for camping, as it afforded shelter from the desert and mountain winds. At its base the ground is wet and is used today as a watering place for range cattle.

297. Fifteen and six-tenths miles.

✠

SAN ELEUTERIO–
SANTA BÁRBARA
OCTOBER 11–OCTOBER 21

October 11

On the 11th we left San Eleuterio on a south-by-east course. We let the companions go ahead so that we two could go on discussing the means we ought to take, and the ones best suited, to remove from our companions—especially Don Bernardo Miera, Don Joaquín Laín, and Andrés Muñiz the interpreter—the extreme dissatisfaction with which they were abandoning the trip to Monterey and were following this one, which for the present we deemed expedient and according to God's most holy will, for Whom we solely wanted to travel and were ready to suffer and, if need be, to die. We had already disclosed to them at Santa Brígida the reasons for our new resolve, and instead of paying heed to their validity they were setting their views against ours.

And so, from this place onward, they came along very peevishly; everything was extremely onerous, and all unbearably irksome. Their conversations had no other topic than the negative results they would derive from such a lengthy trip, because for them it did not consist in having discovered such a great deal of country and people so well disposed to be easily gathered into the Lord's vineyard and to the realms of his majesty (whom God keep), nor in having come to know such widespread provinces heretofore unknown, nor finally in already having one soul assured to the Church's bosom. This gain is a greater reward and worth the longest journeys, the greatest hardships and fatigues—and besides, we had already overcome many handicaps for going to Monterey later on.

But they listened to none of this, for the first one of those here mentioned had conceived without any reason whatsoever, at least from our part, grandiose dreams of honors and profit from solely reaching Monterey and had imparted them to the rest by building castles in the air of the loftiest. And now he was assuring them that we had deprived them of these blessings—so grand in their fancy that even the servants

87

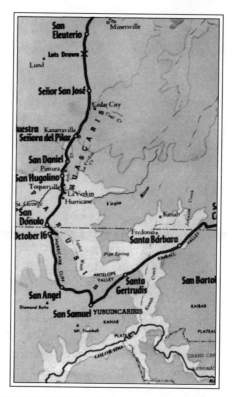

SAN ELEUTERIO TO SANTA BÁRBARA
OCTOBER 11–OCTOBER 21

were giving us plenty to bear. A little before this decision Don Bernardo had been saying that we had advanced but little westward and that we had a great deal of country left before we could reach Monterey, and now he kept on assuring even the servants that we could get there within a week.

Many times before leaving La Villa de Santa Fe we had reminded each and every one of our companions that in this journey we had no other destination than the one which God would grant us; nor did this tempt us to any worldly purpose whatsoever; and that whosoever among them tried either to trade with the infidels or to follow out his private notions by not keeping before him the sole aim of this undertaking, which has been and is God's greater glory and the spreading of the faith, had better not go in our company. On the way we time and again admonished (some) to rectify their intentions, because otherwise we would suffer hardships and misfortunes and would not achieve all that we were aiming for—as they saw in part come true under circumstances which, unless they close their eyes to the Light, they could never attribute to accident. With all this they plagued us more each day, and we were very much disheartened by seeing how in the business of heaven the one of earth was being sought first and foremost.

And so, in order that God's cause stood better justified, and to make them understand more clearly that we had changed our mind neither out of fear nor by our own despotic will, we decided to lay aside altogether the great weight of the arguments mentioned and, after imploring the divine mercy and the intercession of our holy patron saints, to search anew God's will by casting lots—putting *Monterey* on one and *Cosnina* on the other—and to follow the route which came out.[298]

We caught up with the companions[299] and made them dismount. When all were gathered around, Padre Fray Francisco Atanasio set before them the obstacles and difficulties which continuing the trip to Monterey entailed at the time, what we could achieve by going back through Cosnina, finally the blunders and setbacks we might have experienced before this had God not frustrated some of their schemes. He held them responsible for all the evil which could now result by going on to Monterey, especially the desertion and return of Joaquín, the little Laguna. He also let them know that if the lot fell to Monterey there was to be no other leader or guide than Don Bernardo Miera, since he believed it to be so close and everything started from his ideas. Then he gave them a brief exhortation, for them to subject themselves

298. The question of just how they "cast lots" has caused considerable discussion. They probably put the two names in a hat and drew one out. Some believe they write the names on a flat stick and tossed it in the air and followed the route which came out on top. Some cynics have suggested that the two padres, leaving nothing to chance, put two slips in the hat each with the name *Cosnina* on it.

299. Probably at a small hill some two leagues (5.26 miles) due south of Brown Knoll. It has been suggested that this hill be named "Domínguez Dome" after Father Domínguez, who exhorted the travelers here. Presently it is merely identified on the USGS Map as Hill 5343. The fact that it was Father Domínguez who gave the stern lecture and announced the padres' decision concerning the future of the expedition is evidence that it was he who was the actual leader who was faced with announcing the hard decisions to the men.

entirely to God's will and, by laying aside every sort of passion, beg Him with firm hope and lively faith to make it known to us.

They all submitted in a Christian spirit, and with fervent piety prayed the third part of the rosary and other petitions while we ourselves were reciting the Penitential Psalms with the Litany and other orations which follow it. This concluded, we cast lots, and the one of Cosnina came out. This we all heartily accepted now, thanks be to God, mollified and pleased.

We started out again, quickening our pace as much as possible, having come from San Eleuterio ten leagues, two south by east, three south-southeast (already leaving the plain of Nuestra Señora de la Luz), a fourth southeast and a fourth south-southeast, and three and a half southeast of good terrain; then, going through a woods of piñon and juniper along a spreading narrow valley with much pasturage,[300] and afterward some hills fully clad with pastures, we went down into a beautiful valley[301] and halted when it was already dark near a small river on one of its meadows, which are most abundant in pasturage. We named them Valle y Río del Señor San José.[302] Today ten leagues.[303]

A bearing was taken by the North Star, and we found ourselves at 37° 33′ latitude.[304]

THE DIARY AND ITINERARY CONTINUES FROM 37 DEGREES, 33 MINUTES LATITUDE, AND THE ROUTE FROM THE LITTLE RÍO DEL SEÑOR SAN JOSÉ TOWARD EL COLORADO AND COSNINA.

October 12

On the 12th we left the little Río del Señor San José and, because there were some very miry places in it, we went across a big marsh with much water and pasturage, through the middle of which another par-

---

300. Horse Hollow appears to be the route taken, rather than the Mud Springs area as described by Bolton. Horse Hollow can be seen from "Domínguez Dome," whereas Mud Springs does not present a passable canyon from that point. They would have headed for the obvious break in the mountains as observed from Domínguez Dome, that is, Horse Hollow.

301. Cedar Valley.

302. Located in a pasture about eleven miles north of Cedar City on a dry streambed which was formerly called Coal Creek. The journal calls this the Valley and River of Lord Saint Joseph—referring to the spouse of the Virgin Mary.

303. Twenty-six and three-tenths miles.

304. About 37° 50′. In this instance they were somewhat low in their calculations.

cel of water flows as though it were an irrigation ditch. Then, after crossing it in a northwesterly direction, we swung straight south along the western side of the plain's meadows, and after going four leagues and a half over good terrain we saw that the companions, who were going some distance ahead of us, hastily left the trail. We hurried up to learn the cause, and when we caught up with them they were already talking with two Indian women whom they had detained by force because, on seeing them, the latter had started to run away with other ones, up to twenty perhaps, who had been gathering wild plant seeds on the plain.

It pained us to see them frightened so much that they could not even speak, and we tried to take away their fear and misgivings through the interpreter and Joaquín the Laguna. After having recovered somewhat, they told us that there were many people of their kind in this vicinity, that they had heard it said that toward the south they wore blue clothing and that El Río Grande was not very far from here. We could not clearly draw out from them from what nation these blue garments or fabrics came nor hazard a guess about this from what they said, because we knew that only red materials arrive among the Payuchis. But then it occurred to us that the Cosninas buy short blue blouses of wool in Moqui, and so we concluded that they were speaking of the latter. From this we inferred that we were already near El Río Colorado and Cosnina.

These Indian women were so poorly dressed that they wore only some pieces of deerskin hanging from the waist, barely covering what one cannot gaze upon without peril. We sent them away, telling them to notify their people that we came in peace, that we harmed no one, that we loved everybody—and so, for the men who were able, to come without misgivings to the place where we were going to spend the night. We continued over the plain and valley of Señor San José, and after going south for three more leagues saw other Indians who were running away. We dispatched the interpreter with Joaquín the Laguna and another companion to try to bring one of them back to the halting place which we were approaching, in order to inquire if El Río Grande was close by as the Yuta women had insisted and to see if one of them wanted to accompany us as a guide to Cosnina. They were running so fast that they were barely able to get hold of one. Don Joaquín Laín brought him riding hind-saddle on his horse to where we had already stopped, after we had gone south another half a league next to a small stream, which we named Río de Nuestra Señora del Pilar de

Zaragoza,[305] where there was plenty of good pasturage as in the entire valley. Today eight leagues[306] south.

This Indian, whom we have been saying our companions brought to the king's camp, was overly vivacious, and so intimidated that he appeared to be out of his mind. He stared in every direction, watched everyone closely, and any gesture or motion on our part startled him beyond measure. Then, to escape what his excessive timidity suspected, he paid so close attention when we spoke to him, and answered so quickly, that he seemed to anticipate the questions rather than grasp them. He calmed down, and we gave him something to eat and a ribbon which we ourselves put on him. He carried a large, well-fashioned hempen net which he said he used for catching jackrabbits and cottontails. When we asked him from where they brought those nets, he answered that they came from other Indians who live down El Río Grande, from where also, we later learned, they brought the colorful shells—and, according to the distance and direction in which he assigned them, they appear to be the Cocomaricopas.[307] With respect to the distance to El Río Grande, and to the blue clothing, he said the same thing as the Indian women, adding that some strands of dyed wool that he carried he had bought this summer from two of those wearing the blue clothing mentioned who had crossed the river.

We questioned him in different ways where the Cosninas were, but he gave us no clue concerning them, either because these ones call them by another name, or perhaps because he figured that if he admitted knowing them we would forcibly take him along to lead us to them, or finally because he didn't know them. We asked him if he had heard it said that toward the west or northwest, pointing in these directions, there were padres and Spaniards, and he answered that there weren't any, that although many peoples lived all over these areas, these were of his very own language, and Indians like himself. They showed him a kernel of maize, and he then said that he had seen how it was culti-

305. The line of travel took the party southward through Cedar Valley, west of the Cross Hollow Hills, and east of Quichapa Lake toward the headwaters of Kanarra Creek, a tributary of Ash Creek, which is located in a narrow valley between the Cedar and the Harmony mountains. The campsite of Our Lady of the Pilar of Zaragoza is located on present Kanarra Creek about 20 miles south of the Señor San José campsite, about 10 miles south of Cedar City, and about 1¼ miles west-northwest of the town of Kanarraville.

306. Twenty and eight-tenths miles.

307. They lived along the left bank of the Gila River in Arizona.

vated, and that at a camp which we would reach next day there was a little of this grain they had brought from where it was raised. We made considerable efforts to get him to declare what people these were who planted the latter, and other things about which he gave a confusing account, and all that we could draw out is that they lived on this side of El Río Grande next to another small river. He willingly stayed all night with us and promised to take us to the camp mentioned.

October 13

On the 13th we set out southward from the rivulet and stopping point of Nuestra Señora del Pilar, accompanied by the Indian mentioned, to whom we had promised a big all-purpose knife so that he would guide us until we encountered others. We traveled south for two leagues and a half and came to the camp mentioned ahead, which was his own. In it there were a very old Indian, a young man, several children, and three women, and all of them handsome. They had very good piñon nuts, yucca dates, and some little pouches of maize. We conversed with the old one a long while, but he told us no more than the previous ones. We gave the promised knife to the one who had led us there and suggested that, if any one of the three wished to accompany us to those who they said planted the maize, we would pay them well.

From the reply we learned that they still suspected us very much and feared us a great deal, but on the companions' suggestion we placed before them a large all-purpose knife and some beads of white glass. Prompted by his great suspicion, the old man seized it and offered himself as our guide in order to get us out of there, as it later became evident to us, so as to allow time for his family to get away and retreat to the nearby sierra. We went on our way, accompanied by the said ancient individual and the other one who had spent the preceding night with us.

We traveled south for a league and a half, went down to the little Río del Pilar,[308] which here has a leafy poplar grove, crossed it as we now left El Valle del Señor San José, and entered a ridge-cut entirely of black lava rock which lies between two high sierras by way of a gap.[309] In the roughest part of this cut the two guides vanished from our sight,

308. Down the Kanarra Creek, which now becomes Ash Creek.
309. Through Ash Creek Canyon.

so that we never saw them again. We applauded their cleverness in having brought us through a place so well suited for carrying out their ruse so surely and easily. This we had already detected, simply from their great eagerness and the manner in which they agreed to guide us. Bereft of a guide, we continued south for a league with great hardship on account of so much rock, went down a second time to the said Río del Pilar, and halted by its edge and a pleasant poplar grove, naming the place San Daniel.[310] Today five leagues[311] south.

El Valle del Señor San José, which we finished crossing, lies in its northernmost part at 37° 33′ latitude and is nearly twelve leagues from north to south, and from east to west more than three in places, in others two, and in others less. It greatly abounds in pasturelands, has large meadows and middling marshes, and very fine land sufficient for a good settlement for dry-farming because, although it has no water for irrigating more than some land by the rivulets of San José and El Pilar, the great moisture of the terrain can supply this lack without irrigation being missed; for the moisture throughout the rest of the valley is so great that not only the meadows and lowlands but even the elevations now had pastures as green and as fresh as the most fertile of river meadows during the months of June and July.

Very close to its circumference there is a great source of timber and firewood of ponderosa pine and piñon, and good sites for raising large and small livestock. The Indians who inhabit it and parts adjacent to it along the west, north, and east, call themselves Huascari in their language. They dress very poorly, eat wild plant seeds, jackrabbits, piñon nuts in season, and yucca dates. Maize they do not plant, and they acquire very little of it as we saw. They are extremely low-spirited, and different from the Lagunas and from the Barbones [full-bearded ones]. They border on the latter along the northwest and north and employ their language, although with some variation. At this place of San Daniel ends the country of the Lagunas, which extends from El Valle de las Salinas directly south to here; and from here to El Río Grande it is all mesa-strewn land, and it shows signs of having many minerals.

---

310. Saint Daniel campsite is located about 2.4 miles north of the Pintura Interchange and 3/4 mile north of the Snowfield Interchange on Interstate 15. It is in a clearing on the west side of Ash Creek.

311. Slightly over 13 miles.

October 14

On the 14th we set out from San Daniel, going south by west along the west side of the river,[312] getting away somewhat from it, and, after going two leagues over hills of very brilliant white sand and plenty of rock cliffs in places, we crossed two most copious springs of good water which flow into the river mentioned ahead. We swung to the south, now over rock of malpais (which is like volcanic slag, although heavier and less porous) and not too troublesome, now in between sandstone cliffs or else along sandy shelves, and after going two more leagues went down a third time to the river and halted by its edge, naming the stopping place, where there was good pasturage, San Hugolino.[313]

Here it is already very temperate country for, in spite of our having experienced plenty of heat yesterday, last night, and today, the river poplars were so green and leafy, the flowers and blooms which the land produces so flamboyant and without damage whatsoever, that they indicated there had been no freezing or frosting around here. We also saw growths of mesquite, which does not flourish in very cold lands. Today four leagues south.

October 15

On the 15th we left San Hugolino along the river's west side and along the slope of some adjacent hills, and after going south-southwest for two leagues and a half we returned to the river's edge and poplar grove. Here we found a well-constructed primitive arbor with plenty of ears and shocks of maize which had been placed on top. Close to it, on the brief bottoms and bank of the river, were three small maize fields with their well-dug irrigation ditches. The stalks of maize which they had harvested this year were still standing. We were particularly overjoyed by this, both on account of the hope it gave us of being able to provide ourselves with familiar provisions farther ahead, and more importantly because it furnished evidence of these peoples' practice of agriculture—and to find all this in an advanced stage for reducing it to civil ways of living and to the faith whenever the Most High so disposes.

For by now it is known how much there is entailed in accustoming the other Indians to this, and how much their conversion is made

---

312. That is, on the west side of the Río de Pilar, or Ash Creek.
313. Just west of Ash Creek, within the boundaries of the town of Toquerville, Utah, about two blocks due west of the old Mormon chapel.

difficult by their aversion to this labor so necessary for living primarily in civil ways and in towns. From here downstream and on the mesas on either side for a long stretch, according to what we learned, live these Indians who apply themselves to cultivating maize and squash, and in their language call themselves Parussis.

We continued south downstream,[314] and after going half a league swung to the southwest, getting away from the river; but a tall embankment without any descent made us backtrack more than a quarter of a league until we returned to the river, which here flows southwest. Here two other tiny rivers enter it, one which comes from the north-north-east,[315] and the other from the east. The latter consists of hot and sulphurous waters, for which we named it Río Sulfúreo.[316] Here there is a beautiful grove of black poplars, some willow trees, and rambling vines of wild grape. Over the space where we backtracked there are ash-strewn areas, veins and other mineral indications, and many rocks smeared with mica.

We crossed El Río del Pilar and El Sulfúreo near where they join, and going south we climbed a low mesa between outcroppings of black and shiny rock. After climbing it we got onto good open country and crossed a brief plain which has a chain of very tall mesas to the east, and to the west hills with sagebrush (what in Spain is heather) and red sand. On the plain we could have taken the edge of the cliffs and ended our day's march on good and level land, but those who were going ahead changed course in order to follow some fresh tracks of Indians, and they took us over the hills and low sandy places mentioned, where our mounts became very much exhausted.[317]

Over them we went three leagues to the southwest (after previously traveling two other leagues south across the mesa and plain mentioned). We turned south a little more than two leagues and got a view of a short valley surrounded by mesas, on one of which we found ourselves unable to descend to the valley. There was neither water nor pasturage on it for the horse herds, and so we were obliged to go down a rough and very rocky high ridge;[318] then, having gone three-quarters of

314. Still on Ash Creek.
315. The La Verkin River.
316. "Sulphur River," known today as the Virgin River. The La Verkin Hot Springs are located just upstream from Hurricane, Utah.
317. This day the party passed just west of present Hurricane and on to Sand Mountain. The major problem here was the means of descending it.
318. Possible to descend but very treacherous.

a league south, we halted, by the time the sun had set, in an arroyo were we found good and large waterholes with sufficient pasturage for the horse herd. We named the place San Dónulo, or Arroyo del Taray[319] [tamarisk], because here there were trees or growth of this designation. Today ten leagues,[320] which in a straight line would be seven[321] south by west. We took a bearing by the North Star and found ourselves at 36° 52′ 30″ latitude.[322]

On this plain or small valley, besides the tamarisk, there is a good deal of fetid wild rue, the spring leaves of which are very curative, as learned by experience in New Mexico. Tonight our provisions ran out completely, with nothing left but two little slabs of chocolate for to-morrow.

October 16

On the 16th we left San Dónulo with the intention of continuing south as far as El Río Colorado; but shortly after we set out we heard people shouting behind us, and, turning around to see where the repeated sounds came from, we saw eight Indians atop the little bluffs at the stopping point we had just left. These are situated on the plain's middle, extending almost all the way across it and abounding in transparent gypsum and mica. We went back to them, ordering the interpreter, who was going ahead, to come also. We reached the base of the bluff and advised them to come down without fear because we came in peace and were friends. This encouraged them and they came down, showing us for barter some strings of native turquoise, each one having a vari-colored conch shell.[323] This puzzled us for the nonce, because from below they looked to us like rosaries, and the shells like saints' medals.

We stayed here with them a short while, but they speak Yuta so differently from all the rest that neither the interpreter nor Joaquín the Laguna could make them understand them fully, nor these compre-

319. San Dónulo, or Arroyo del Taray (Tamarisk), is located just south of the Utah-Arizona border in Arizona. It is where Hurricane Wash cuts through a low hogback. It was on this hogback where the Indians were found "on the hills near the campsite."

320. Twenty-six and three-tenths miles.

321. Eighteen and four-tenths miles.

322. Actually 37°. Utah-Arizona border, 1/4 mile into Arizona.

323. A little shell from the seacoast, used by the Indians for necklaces and ornaments. White, pink, and black shells were especially prized by the Indians, who intermingled the colors for contrast.

hend most of what they were saying. Nonetheless, either by signs or because in some things they spoke Yuta more like the Lagunas, we understood them to say that they were all Parussis (except one who spoke more of a gibberish than Yuta, and we judged to be Jomajaba)[324] and that they were the ones who farm on the banks of El Río del Pilar and live downstream for a long distance. We took them for Cosninas, but later we found out that they were not. They offered to trade their turquoises, and when we told them that we had nothing there for bartering and that, if they so wished, they could come with us until we overtook the rest of our companions, when we would give them what they asked and would talk more at length with them, they all came along very cheerfully—but those who were more cautious with great fear and misgivings.

We made a halt and talked for more than two hours and a half or three hours. They told us that in two days we would reach El Río Grande,[325] but that we could not go by the route we intended because there were no water sources, nor could we cross the river by this route for its being very much boxed in and very deep, and having extremely tall rocks and cliffs along both sides, and finally that between here and the river there was very bad terrain. We presented them with two large all-purpose knives, and each individual with a string of white glass beads. Then we suggested to them that if any one of them wanted to lead us to the river we would pay him. They answered that they would go along and set us on our way through a canyon which lay at the mesa east of the plain, and that from there we could make it alone, since they were barefoot and could not walk very far.

We did not want to give up going south toward the river, no matter what this information, for we suspected that the Moquis might have come to be at odds with the Cosninas for their having escorted Padre Garcés to them, and that they, fearing that we might again bring other padres and Spaniards into Moqui, had tried to restrain them with threats—and the news having spread about, these ones were now trying to lead us astray so that we would not reach the Cosninas or their neighbors, the Jomajabas. But at the insistence of all the companions, to whom revealing our suspicion did not suit us at present, we consented to take the canyon route.

324. The Mojave Indians.
325. The Río Grande referred to here is the Colorado River. The name "Big River" was applied by the Spaniards rather indiscriminately to almost any large river.

We offered these Indians soles from the hide of hampers as footwear, so that they would guide us. They said that two could go with us until they set us on a correct and proper route. We entered the aforesaid canyon with them and went through it for a league and a half with extremest difficulty and obstruction for the horse herds, because of the presence of so much rubble, flint, and recurring difficult and dangerous stretches. We came to a narrow defile[326] so bad that it took us more than half an hour to get only three saddle mounts through. This was followed by a cliff-filled incline[327] so ruggedly steep that even climbing it on foot would be most difficult.

When the Indians saw that we could not follow them they ran off, prompted no doubt by their mean timidity. This made it necessary for us to backtrack in order to take to the south once more. Before doing this we stopped a while for the horses to regain some strength and drink of the water that was here but so bad that many of the mounts refused to drink. In the afternoon we backtracked through the entire canyon, and after going south half a league along the plain we halted near the valley's southern pass, without water for ourselves and for the horse herd. Tonight we were in direst need, with nothing by way of food, and so we decided to deprive a horse of its life so as not to forfeit our own; but because there was no water we postponed carrying it out until the place where there would be some. Today, in so painful a day's march, we only advanced one league and a half[328] south.

October 17

On the 17th we continued south on our way, went through the little valley's gap mentioned along the box channel of an arroyo, where we found a good waterhole and the entire horse herd drank. We traveled south for two leagues, and, after swinging southeast for another two, found a great quantity of good water in another arroyo, not merely in one spot but in many. And even though it is rainwater, what is left from the freshets, it does not seem to waste away throughout the entire year. Here we came upon some of the [edible] weeds that are called

---

326. Rock Canyon.
327. In the upper portion of Rock Canyon.
328. Camp was in rocky Cottonwood Wash, just beyond the point where this wash emerges from the Hurricane Cliffs. They camped just to the east of Hurricane Wash. They were in such dire straits and so tired, hungry, and disappointed after this day's travel that they neglected to honor this campsite with a name. They made less than four miles' progress that day.

quelites.[329] We thought we might supply our most urgent need with them, but we could gather only a very few, and these tiny.

We continued southeast and, after going four leagues and a half over level and good terrain, although somewhat spongy, we halted, both to see if there was water in the mesa's drainings and to provide some nourishment from the weeds mentioned for Don Bernardo Miera, since he—as we had not eaten a thing since yesterday morning—came so weakened already that he could barely talk. We had the leather hampers and the other luggage searched, in which we had brought our food supplies, to see if there were some leftovers, and we only found some pieces of squash which the servants had obtained yesterday from the Parussi Indians[330] and had hidden to avoid having to share them with the rest. With this and a bit of brown sugarloaf which we also found, we made a concoction for everybody and took some nourishment. We found no water to help us pass the night here and decided to continue our day's march south.

The companions, without letting us know, went to reconnoiter the east mesa and terrain which went on from here. Those who went on this scouting came back saying that the mesa's ascent was very good and that beyond it came flat country with many arroyos where there had to be good water and that they figured the river to be at the end of the plain lying beyond the mesa. With this, all were for changing course. We well knew that they were fooling themselves as on other occasions, and that they could not have seen so much in so short a time; and we held a contrary opinion because toward the south we had a great deal of good level land in sight, and today we had found so much water, in contrast to the Indians' story, and had made the whole day's march over good country, so that our aforementioned suspicion kept on growing.

But since we now found ourselves without provisions, and the water could be far away—and lest carrying out our notion made the thirst and hunger we might encounter on either route more intolerable for them—we told them (for our sake) to choose the way that suited them best. They took us over the mesa toward the southeast, climbing it through a rough wash or very rocky arroyo in which there is very good gypsum rock of the kind used for whitewashing. We finished climbing

329. This was a common name given to various types of plants in Mexico which were eaten as greens, as in salads.
330. The Shivwit Indians. Also spelled "Parusis" in the journal.

the mesa over a quite steep slope and a great deal of black rock. Night fell, and we halted atop the mesa on a short plain of good pasturage but without water, naming it San Ángel.[331] Today nine leagues.[332]

We were very sorry for having changed direction because, according to the latitude in which we were, we could have reached the river very quickly by going south. As soon as we stopped, those who had been on the mesa before told us that a short distance from here they thought that they had seen water. Two went off to bring some for the men, but they did not return all night, and the next day dawned without our having heard from them. Of course, we concluded that they had gone ahead looking for Indian camps where they could relieve their privation as soon as possible. For this reason, and because there was no water here, we decided to go on without waiting for them.

October 18

On the 18th we set out from San Ángel toward the east-southeast, and, after going half a league, turned east by south for two leagues over spreading hills and narrow valleys, well pastured but with a great deal of rock; and not finding water, we turned east by north for two more leagues, going up and down hills of a kind of rock which was very troublesome for the horse herds. There were five Indians peering at us from a short but high mesa; as we two, who were coming behind the companions, passed along its base, they spoke to us. When we turned toward where they were, four of them hid themselves and only one stayed in sight. We realized the great fear they had; we could not persuade him to come down, and we two went up on foot with plenty of trouble. At each step we took, as we came closer to him, he wanted to take off. We let him know that he did not have to be afraid, that we loved him like a son and wanted to talk with him. And so he waited for us, making a thousand gestures to show that he feared us very much.

As soon as we climbed up to where he was, we embraced him, and

331. From the October 16 campsite the party headed south along Hurricane Wash with the towering Hurricane Cliffs on their left. They closely paralleled the Old Temple Road built by the Mormons almost a century later to haul timber eighty miles from Mount Trumbull to St. George for the construction of the temple. They threaded the narrow two-mile-long Black Canyon, formed by an extensive lava flow, and then continued south and then southeast over good open country near the base of the Hurricane Cliffs until they reached the point where the Temple Trail later ascended these cliffs. From the crest the route led into a shallow valley that is thickly covered with grass and good pasturage, but no water. They camped here.

332. A little over 23.5 miles.

on seating ourselves beside him we had the interpreter and the Laguna come up. Now composed, he said that the other four were hiding over yonder, that he would call them if we wished, so that we could see them. When we told him that we did, he laid his arrows and bow upon the ground, took the interpreter by the hand, and they went to fetch them. They came over, we talked for about an hour, and they told us that we already had water close at hand. We begged them to come along and show it to us, promising them a swatch of woolen cloth, and after much urging three of them consented to go with us. We went on with them, very much exhausted from thirst and hunger, for a league toward the southeast and after going another to the south over a bad and very rocky route, we came to a juniper wood and an arroyo which harbored two large waterholes within its deep recesses. We drew out enough for ourselves and brought over the horse herd, which, for coming so thirsty, drained both pools. Here we decided to spend the night, naming the site San Samuel.³³³ Today six leagues.³³⁴

The three Indians mentioned who came with us were so scared that they did not want to go farther, nor let us come near them, until they questioned Joaquín the Laguna, and they calmed down with what he told them about us. Among other things they asked him, very much impressed by his valor, was how it happened that he had dared to come with us. He, in his desire to take away their fear in order to relieve the privation he was suffering to our sorrow, answered them as best he could at the time. And so he relieved them of much of the fear and suspicion which they still felt, this no doubt being the reason why they did not leave us before we reached the water source mentioned.

As soon as we camped we gave them the woolen stuff that we promised, with which they were greatly pleased. Then, when they learned that we came without food supplies, they told us to have one of our own go over with one of theirs to their humble abodes, which were somewhat distant, and to bring some back—that the others would remain with us in the meantime. We sent one of the mixed-breeds along with Joaquín the Laguna, giving them the wherewithal for buying pro-

333. At the mouth of Bobcat Canyon. This canyon, on an upper headstream of Clayhole Wash, is about two miles long, leading north from Bobcat Reservoir through a long lava ridge. The camp was undoubtedly made at the mouth of the canyon near several pools of water that had collected on the bedrock streambed. The camp, located two miles south of Swapp Reservoir, was occupied by the Spaniards for the nights of October 18 and 19. This site is known to local ranchers as "Cooper's Pockets."
334. That is, 15.78 miles.

visions and a pack horse on which to bring them. They left with the other Indian and returned after midnight, bringing back a small quantity of wild sheep meat, dried cactus prickly pear done into cakes, and seeds from wild plants. They also brought news about one of the two who had gone for water the night before, saying that he had been at the camp. The other had arrived tonight before ten.

October 19
On the 19th, twenty of these Indians came to the king's camp with some cactus pear in cakes or dough, and several pouches of seeds from different plants, for us to purchase from them. We paid them for everything they brought, and we charged them to bring meat, piñon nuts, and more cactus pear if they had any, that we would buy it all, especially the meat. They said they would, but that we had to wait for them until noon. We accepted the condition and they went away. One of them had consented to accompany us as far as the river if we waited until the afternoon, and we likewise agreed. In the afternoon many more came over than those who had been with us previously, and among them one who they said was a Mescalero Apache[335] and who had come with two others from their country to this one, having crossed the river a few days before. He had very unpleasant features and differed from these Indians in his dislike of seeing us around here and, as we noticed, in the great animosity which he purposely displayed. They said that these Apaches were friends of theirs.

They did not bring any meat, but they did bring many leather pouches of the seeds mentioned, and some fresh cactus pears already ripened in the sun, and others dried in cakes. We bought from them about a bushel of seeds and all the cactus pears, talked a long while about the distance to the river, the route toward it, their own numbers and mode of living, about the neighboring peoples, and concerning the guide we were asking for. They showed us which way to go to the river, furnishing a few vague directions with regard to the ford, and saying that we would get there in two or three days. They told us that they called themselves Yubuincariri,[336] that they did not plant maize, that the only foods were those seeds, cactus pears, the piñon nuts—of which they gather very few, judging from the little they had—and

335. Called "mescal people," from their custom of eating mescal. They inhabited the mountains near the Pecos River in the eighteenth century.
336. Also spelled "Yubuincariris" in the journal. These are Uinkarits, a band of the Paiute tribe.

whatever jackrabbits, cottontails, and wild sheep they hunted, adding that on this side only the Parussis planted maize and squash, but that on the other side, just across the river, there were the Ancamuchis[337] (whom we understood to be the Cosninas), and that these planted a lot of maize. Besides these, they gave the names of other peoples, their neighbors along the south-southwest on this western side of the river, these being the Payatammunis.[338] They also informed us of the Huascaris,[339] whom we had already seen in El Valle del Señor San José.

As to the Spaniards of Monterey, not even the least indication of their having heard them spoken of. One of those who had spent the previous night with us informed us that he had heard about the journey of the Reverend Padre Garcés;[340] this, together with the denial by all these others of knowing the Cosninas (unless they know them by the name "Ancamuchi," given above), seems to prove that we already mentioned having suspected. When the talk came to an end they started leaving, without our being able to get one of them to decide to accompany us as far as the river.

Today Don Bernardo Miera was very sick to his stomach, and so we could not set out from here this afternoon. And a little farther away we found other waterholes for tonight.

October 20

On the 20th we set out from San Samuel toward the north-northeast, directing our way to the ford of El Río Colorado, and, after ignoring a low, wooded, and very rocky sierra that lies on this side, and having gone a little more than two leagues, we swung northeast and came onto flat country without rock; then, after traveling four leagues, we found several banked pools of good water in an arroyo. After going one league east-northeast, we halted by its edge between two bluffs which stand on the plain close to the arroyo, where they was a great supply of water and good pasturage. We named this place Santa Gertrudis,[341]

337. The Cosnina, known as the Havasupai today.
338. Also spelled "Payatanumis" in the journal.
339. The Cedar Indians.
340. Elliott Coues, ed. and trans., *On The Trail of a Spanish Pioneer: The Diary and Itinerary of Francisco Garcés, 1775–76*, 2 vols. (New York: F. P. Harper, 1900).
341. "Saint Gertrude." On Bull Rush Wash, at a point where the two sides of the hogback appear as bluffs. The breaks of the hogback are very prominent in an area which is practically a plain, and the campsite can be fixed positively. Like nearly all streams in the Strip Country, Bull Rush Wash has been deeply entrenched. This is clearly evident at Santa Gertrudis, where the arroyo is twenty feet deep.

observing its latitude by the North Star, which is 36° 30′.[342] Today seven leagues.[343]

October 21

On the 21st we set out from Santa Gertrudis, headed east, and after going half a league we turned northeast. Several times we crossed El Arroyo de Santa Gertrudis,[344] which in most places had large banked ponds of water; then, having traveled five leagues and a half northeast over not too good terrain and some twists and turns, we went over sagebrush stretches which were not troublesome and over good terrain. Then, after going a little more than four leagues east-northeast, we halted when it was already dark near a small ravine with good pasturage, but lacking water even for the men. Lorenzo de Olivares, driven by thirst for having eaten too many of the seeds, piñon nuts, and cactus pears we had bought, went off as soon as we stopped in order to look for water in the arroyos nearby and did not make an appearance all night; this caused us plenty of worry. Today ten leagues.[345] We named the place Santa Bárbara.[346]

342. Somewhat higher than their calculations. They were closer to 36° 59′ at this point.

343. Almost 18.5 miles.

344. Bull Rush Wash. When they later crossed Kanab Creek, they did not describe it, which appears rather strange.

345. Twenty-six and three-tenths miles.

346. Located about five miles southeast of Fredonia, Arizona, in Johnson Wash (sometimes called Kimball Valley).

SANTA BÁRBARA–ORAIBI
OCTOBER 22–NOVEMBER 16

October 22

On the 22nd we left Santa Bárbara and headed north-northeast looking for the said Olivares. About two leagues away we found him near a scanty pool of water which only provided enough for the men to drink, and for a small barrel we brought along in case we came upon water tonight. We continued over the plain and, after going four leagues northeast, saw a path which went south; then, when the interpreter said that the Yubuincariris had told him that this was the one we had to take to reach the river, we took it; but, after following it one league south, we found that the interpreter was ambiguous about the signs, because the path mentioned turned back after a short distance. And so, heading east, we went up the low sierra we had been trying to avoid, which stretched almost from north to south all across the eastern side of the plain. We crossed it with plenty of difficulty and fatigue experienced by the horse herds, because it was very rocky besides having many gulches.[347]

Night overtook us while we were descending on the other side along a very high ridge, steep and full of rubble. From it we saw several fires below, beyond a short plain. We thought that Andrés the interpreter and Joaquín the Laguna, who had gone ahead looking for water for tonight, had built them to let us know where they were. But, after we had finished descending and gone five leagues east-northeast upon leaving the path mentioned, making some detours in the sierra's ravines, we came to the fires where there were three tiny camps of Indians, and with them our interpreter and Joaquín. We decided to spend the night here since a little distance away to the east and west there was water and pasturage for the horse herd, which by now was almost to-

---

347. The Kaibab Plateau. The expedition crossed the plateau from west to east during this day's march.

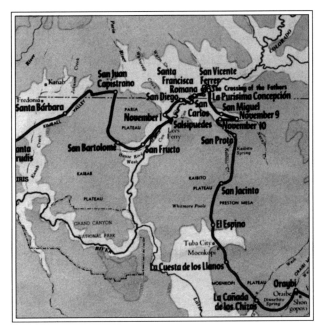

SANTA BÁRBARA TO ORAIBI, OCTOBER 22–NOVEMBER 16

tally spent, naming the place San Juan Capistrano.[348] Today twelve
leagues.[349]

Since it was already dark when we reached these camps, and the
Indians could not make out the number of people coming, they became so much alarmed that, in spite of the pleadings of the interpreter
and Joaquín the Laguna, most of them ran away as we arrived, only
three men and two women remaining behind. Greatly worried, the latter were saying to our Laguna, "Little brother, you belong to our very
own kind; do not let these people with whom you come kill us."

We treated them all fondly and tried by every possible means we
could think of to rid them of the suspicion and fear they bore us. They
calmed down a bit, and in an effort to please us presented us with two
roasted jackrabbits and some piñon nuts. Two of them, although very
much afraid, went to show the servants where the horse herd could

348. At, or very near, Coyote Spring. There is no other spring water north or
south for several miles. The camp was on the sandy benches east-northeast of the
spring a short distance from and about a hundred feet above the bed of Coyote Wash.
This is in Arizona.

349. Thirty-one and a half miles.

drink. This place is located east of the northern point of the little sierra mentioned, close to a number of small red earthen mounts.
South of these, very near, on the top of some cliffy hills with some
piñon and juniper trees, are two good deposits of rainwater. Closer to
them in a small arroyo there are some waterholes also, but here
scanty and not as good. To the west-southwest from the same little
bluffs at the sierra's base there is also a little spring of permanent
water.

These Indians are called Pagampachi[350] in their language, and their
immediate neighbors along the north and northwest, Ytimpabichi.[351]

After we had retired to rest, some of the companions, Don Bernardo Miera among them, went to one of the huts to chat with the
Indians. They told them that the said Don Bernardo had been sick all
along, and one old Indian from among those present, either because
our own requested it or on his own accord, set about to cure him with
chants and ceremonials which, if not overt idolatries (which they had
to be), were wholly superstitious. All of our own gladly permitted
them, the sick man included, and they hailed them as indifferent
kindly gestures when they should have prevented them for being contrary to the evangelical and divine law which they profess, or at least
they should have withdrawn. We heard the Indian's chanting, but did
not know what it was all about. As soon as they gave us a detailed account next morning, we were extremely grieved by such harmful carelessness and we reprimanded them, instructing them in doctrine so
that they would never again lend their approval to such errors through
their willing attendance or in any other manner.

This is one of the main reasons why the infidels who have most
dealings with the Spaniards and Christians in these parts show more
resistance to the truth of the Gospel, and their conversion becomes
more difficult each day. While we were preaching the necessity of holy
baptism to the first Sabuaganas we saw, the interpreter, so as not to
displease them or else lose the friendship of long standing which they
maintain with them through the despicable fur trade (even in the face
of just prohibitions by the lord governors of this kingdom, who time
and again have decreed that no Indian, mixed-breed Indian, or Hispanic settler many enter infidel country without first having obtained

---

350. The Kaibab band of the Paiute Indians.
351. The Timpeabits, a Paiute band.

permission for it from his lordship),[352] translated for them in these very words: "The padre says that the Apaches, Navajos, and Comanches who are not baptized cannot enter heaven, and that they go to hell where God punishes them, and they will burn forever like wood in the fire"—and with this the Sabuaganas became overjoyed on hearing themselves excluded, and their foes included, in the unavoidable destiny of either being baptized or of being lost forever. The interpreter was reprimanded, and he changed his conduct on seeing his stupid puny faith exposed.

We could add other examples, heard from those very ones who while among the Yutas have attended and perhaps approved and even participated in many idolatrous practices; but the two just related, to which we bear witness, suffice. For, if in our company, after having heard these idolatries and superstitions repeatedly being refuted and condemned, they attend them, furnish occasion for them, and applaud them, what will they not do while wandering three or four months among the infidel Yutas and Navajos with no one to correct them or restrain them?

Besides this, they (some of them) have furnished us sufficient reasons during this trip to suspect that, when some go to the Yutas and remain among them in their greed for pelts, others go after the flesh which they find here for their bestial satisfaction. And so, therefore, they blaspheme against Christ's name and impede or, to put it better, oppose the spreading of the faith. Oh, with how much severity should similar evils be attended to! May God in His infinite goodness inspire the most suitable and practical means.

October 23

On the 23rd we undertook no day's march, to give those from around here a chance to calm down and those of the surrounding area to come over. The wild plant seeds and other foodstuffs we had bought and eaten made us quite sick, weakening us instead of giving us nourishment. We could not get these people to sell us any of the usual meat, and so we had a horse slaughtered and the flesh prepared for taking along.

352. Repeated *Bandos* or proclamations forbidding trade with the Yutas in this direction to the northwest of Santa Fe are listed in Ralph Emerson Twitchell, *The Spanish Archives of New Mexico*, 2 (1914). See Documents 185 and 740 for examples.

Today Padre Fray Francisco Atanasio was very ill with a severe anal pain, so that he could not even move about.

All day long, Indians kept coming from the adjacent camps, all of whom we treated fondly and entertained as best we could. These now gave us a clearer report about the Cosninas and Moquis, calling them by these very names. They also told us by which way we should go to the river (which is twelve leagues from here at the most), giving us indications about the ford. We bought about a bushel of piñon nuts from them and presented them with more than a half in wild plant seeds.

Very early next day twenty-six Indians came over, some being from among those who were here with us yesterday afternoon, and others whom we had not seen before. We proclaimed the Gospel to them, decrying and explaining to them the wickedness and futility of their evil customs, most especially with regard to the superstitious curing of their sick. We made them understand that they should seek help in their troubles only from the one and true God, because His Majesty alone has power over health and sickness, over life and death, and is able to help everyone. Then, even though our interpreter could not explain this fully to them, one of them—who no doubt had long dealt with the Payuchi Yutas—understood it well and explained what he was hearing to the rest. On seeing how they were listening with pleasure, we proposed to them that, if they wished to become Christians, padres and Spaniards would come to instruct them and live among them. They answered that they did. Then, when we asked them where we could find them on our return, they said it would be on this same sierra and the adjacent mesas.

Finally, to keep building up their affection for us, we distributed three yards of red ribbon among them, giving each one a half, which left them very happy and grateful. One of them had already agreed to go with us as far as the river, so as to direct us to the ford, but when all the others had departed and he had accompanied us for half a league he became so afraid that we could not persuade him to continue. Our thoughtless companions wanted us to make him keep his word by force, but we, understanding his reluctance, let him go freely away.

October 24

On the 24th, about nine in the morning or a little later, we set out from San Juan Capistrano through a narrow valley[353] heading south-south-

353. Up Coyote Wash toward the divide that separates it from House Rock Valley.

east, and after going four leagues we turned southeast within the same valley. Here at the base of the valley's eastern mesa are three runoffs of good water, but there was not enough for the horse herd. From the stopping point to here we traveled over good terrain. After going two more leagues southeast, we swung east-southeast for about three leagues over sandy and troublesome country.[354] And even though we found no water for the horse herd, we stopped on finding pasturage because it was very tired by now, and it was already dark. We named the place San Bartolomé.[355] Here there is extensive valley land but of bad terrain, for what is not sand is a kind of ground having about three inches of rubble, and after that loose soil of different hues. There are many deposits of transparent gypsum, some of mica, and there also seem to be some of metallic ore. Today nine leagues.[356]

Through this area runs El Río Colorado, from north-northeast to south-southwest, very deep inside a canyon, so that even if the land were good the river is of no help for farming near it. This afternoon we saw the embankments and cliffs of the river's box canyon which, when viewed along the western side, give the impression of a lengthy row of structures, but we figured it to be some box canyon of the many arroyos found on the plain.

October 25

On the 25th we set out from San Bartolomé, going east-southeast, and went eastward for one league and less than a half; we did not care to approach near what is actually the box canyon of El Río Grande, because we crossed several arroyos which had canyons as big as its own, and so we concluded that the river did not run through these but through some other arroyo; this is why we turned toward the north-northeastern side of the valley, where we thought we might be able to avoid the mesas that surround it. We took the box channel of an arroyo in search of water for the horse herds, which by now were exhausted from thirst, and, after traveling two leagues northeast through it, we

354. House Rock Valley.
355. The party camped for the night on Emmett Hill, the divide between House Rock Wash and Emmett Wash at a point just to the east of the southernmost point of the Paria Plateau, which towered above them over two thousand feet. The journal mentions soil of different colors. This suggests the many-hued Chinle formation. A patch of Chinle about a quarter of a mile in diameter is to be seen on the surface precisely where the padres made camp. The formation is exposed nowhere else along their trail in this general area.
356. Slightly more than 23.5 miles.

could go no farther, and we got out of it toward the western side by climbing a very bad incline. We took to the north-northeast, and after going two leagues we saw cottonwoods at the mesa's base. We aimed for them and found a good water spring. It had something like saltpeter around its edges; we thought it might be salty water, but on trying it we found it tasted good. We halted here, naming the place San Fructo.[357] Today five leagues.[358]

In the afternoon Don Juan Pedro Cisneros went to explore along the valley's north corner to see if there was a way through and if he could find or catch a glimpse of the river and its ford. He returned after midnight with the welcome news of his now having reached the river, but saying that he did not know if we would be able to get across some mesas and big hogbacks that stood on the other bank. Nevertheless, since he said that the river looked all right to him and had a ford there, we decided to go that way.

October 26

On the 26th we left San Fructo, headed north, traveled three leagues and a half, and came to the place where he previously thought the valley's north exit was;[359] and it turns out to be a corner all hemmed in by very lofty bluffs and big hogbacks of red earth which, for having various formations and the bed below being of the same color, present a pleasingly jumbled scene.[360] We continued in the same direction with excessive difficulty because the horse herds sank up to their knees in the dirt when the surface rubble gave;[361] then, having gone a league and a half, we arrived at El Río Grande de los Cosninas.[362] Here another

357. On Soap Creek in Soap Creek Canyon. Here they found a spring which may still be seen on the right side of the wash about seventy-five feet above the highway bridge. Although there are other springs within a few miles, the distances traveled correspond only with Soap Creek.

358. About 13 miles.

359. The point where they supposed the northern exit of the valley to be was the narrow neck of the valley floor where the Marble Canyon Trading Post and Lodge are located today. Just beyond this point is Navajo Bridge, opened to traffic in 1929.

360. "Jumbled" the country most certainly was, but why it appeared "pleasingly" so to these lost, tired, cold, and hungry travelers is puzzling.

361. Within five miles of Lee's Ferry their route led across a gullied field of disintegrated Moenkopi formation, which was too soft for easy horse travel. Even a traveler on foot sinks a few inches into the dark brown soil with each step. As the journal notes, it is particularly bad when wet.

362. The Colorado River.

small one joins it, which we named Santa Teresa.[363] We crossed this one and halted at the edge of the large one close to a high cliff of gray [tawny?] rock, naming the spot San Benito de Salsipuedes.[364] The entire terrain from San Fructo up to here is very troublesome, and altogether impassable when it contains a little moisture from snow or rain. Today five leagues north.[365]

This afternoon we decided to find out if after crossing the river we could continue from here toward the southeast or east. We were surrounded on all sides by mesas and big hogbacks impossible to climb.[366] To do this, two of those who knew how to swim well entered the river naked with their clothes upon their heads. It was so deep and wide that the swimmers, in spite of their prowess, were barely able to reach the other side, leaving in midstream their clothing, which they never saw again. And since they became so exhausted getting there, nude and barefoot, they were unable to walk far enough to do the said exploring, coming back across after having paused a while to catch their breath.[367]

October 27

On the 27th Don Juan Pedro Cisneros went through the canyon of El Río de Santa Teresa, to see if he could find a passage through it in order to get across the east mesa and return to El Río Grande over more open country where it could be forded by taking advantage of its width, or at least where the horse herd could get across without the danger, which existed here, of its getting buried underneath the waters. He traveled all

363. The Paria River.
364. Crossing the Paria River (Río de Santa Teresa) they camped beside the Colorado River, immediately beneath the precipitous yellow-born ledge of Shinarump Conglomerate, or just downstream from the present boat-launching area at Lee's Ferry. Today their campsite is covered by a dense growth of tamarisk, which has invaded the area largely since 1900. Gazing at the multitude of sheer cliffs about them and at the menacing brown river, they named their campsite San Benito Salsipuedes. A "San Benito" to the New Mexican Franciscan of the eighteenth century referred to a garish white cassock with colored markings worn by errant brothers as a mark of punishment. *Salsipuedes* means "get out if you can." Hence their name for their camp serves as an expression of their pent-up frustrations.
365. About 13 miles.
366. Echo Cliffs and Vermillion Cliffs.
367. That very afternoon they made their first attempt to cross the Colorado by sending some swimmers over. Logically this attempt would have been made about one-quarter mile above their campsite at the mouth of the Paria. This distance would afford ample room to cross above the Paria Rapids and would have permitted them to reach the opposite bank, where it was easy to climb out.

day and part of the night and found no passage. He saw one incline very near here where one might get across the mesa, but it looked too difficult to him. Others went to explore in different directions and found nothing but insuperable obstacles for getting to the ford without retracing much terrain.

October 28

On the 28th we repeated the same attempts, and all in vain. A wood raft was put together in short order, and Padre Fray Silvestre with the servants tried to cross the river by means of it; but since the poles used for pushing it, even though more than five yards long, did not touch bottom a short distance away from shore, it was held back by the waves raised by the contrary wind. And so it thrice came back to the shore it had left, without getting even as far as the river's middle. This, besides being deep and wide, here has quicksands on either bank, in the likes of which we could lose all or the better part of the horse herd.

The Yubuincariri and Pagampachi Indians had assured us that the entire river was very deep except at the ford, for when they went across the water reaches up to the waist or a little more. Because of this, and from other indications they had given us, we guessed that the ford was farther upstream. And so we dispatched Andrés Muñiz and his brother Lucrecio with orders to proceed until they found a place where we could get across the mesa previously mentioned and, when they returned to the river, to look for a good crossing or at least some section where, after we went over by raft, the horse herds could get across without peril.

October 29

On the 29th, not knowing when we would be able to get out of here, and when the meat from the first horse and the piñon nuts and other things we had bought had run out, we ordered another horse killed.

October 30–31

On the 30th and 31st we remained waiting for those who went to look for a ford and a way out.

November 1

On the 1st of November they returned when it was already one in the afternoon, saying that they had found a passage, although a difficult one, and a ford in the river. The way over the mesa was the incline which Cisneros had seen, and, since this was very high and steeply rugged, we decided to get next to it this afternoon. We left the bank of El Río Grande and the distressful Paraje de San Benito de Salsipuedes, went along El Río de Santa Teresa, and, after going a league northwest, halted by its edge at the base of the incline mentioned. Today one league.[368] This afternoon, from sundown to seven in the morning, we were exceedingly cold.

November 2

On the 2nd we left El Río de Santa Teresa and went up the incline, which we named Las Ánimas and which must have been half a league long. It took us more than three hours to climb it because it has a very sloping sand dune for a start, and afterward extremely difficult stretches and most dangerous ledges, and is at the very last impassable. After we had climbed it heading east with utmost difficulty, we went down the other side through cliff-lined gorges as we headed north, and after one league turned east for half a one over a stretch of red sand which was quite troublesome for the horse herds. We ascended a small elevation[369] and, likewise going northeast for two leagues and a half, went down into an arroyo which had water running in places, but brackish even though drinkable. There was also pasturage here, and so we halted in it, naming it San Diego.[370] Today four leagues and a half.[371]

---

368. Only 2.63 miles today up the shallow, winding Paria River. At Lee's Ferry the Shinarump ledge, against which they had camped, forms a vertical escarpment that dips gradually to the north. At the point where this cliff finally disappears at river level is where the ascent was to begin the next day. Camp was made along the Paria at this spot, probably in a nearby grove of cottonwood trees.

369. This difficult climb led to a low spot in the east rim of Paria Canyon. The pass is now known as "Domínguez Pass."

370. Slightly north of the present Arizona-Utah border, although today it lies submerged by two hundred feet of water of Lake Powell. The nearest shore of the lake is the site of the Wahweap Swim Beach.

For the first half mile of this day's travel their route twisted between bleak formations of Chinle shale. This was followed by a steep climb of about 400 vertical feet to a sloping bench covered with large areas of loose red sand. Some of this sand could be avoided, some could not, as they climbed slowly across the bench to the southeast. At a point about 1,000 feet above the Paria the terrain forced them to turn up another very steep slope covered with loose soil and boulders. Finally, about 300 feet from the top, they reached a series of baldrock sandstone ledges that were not only narrow but were dangerously rounded on the outside edge. Switchbacking over and across these ledges, which the journal describes as "impassable," they reached the top through a

Today we stopped about three leagues northeast in a direct line from San Benito de Salsipuedes, close to a multitude of earthen embankments, small mesas, and peaks of red earth which look like ruins of a fortress at first sight.[372]

November 3

On the 3rd we set out from San Diego, headed east-southeast, and after going two leagues came to the river a second time, that is, at the edge of the canyon[373] which here serves as its box channel. The descent to the river is very long, steep, rugged, and precipitous, consisting of such terrible rock embankments that two pack animals which descended the first one could not make it back, even without the equipment. Those who had come by here before had not informed us of this slope, and here we learned that they had not found the ford either, nor in so many days made the necessary exploration of so small a space of terrain, for their having wasted the time looking for those Indians who live hereabouts, and accomplished nothing.

The river was very deep, although not as much as at Salsipuedes, but the horse herds had to swim for a long distance. The good thing about it is that it was not quicksand, either going in or getting out. The companions kept insisting that we should descend to the river, but since there was no way on the other side to go ahead after one crossed the river, except a deep and narrow canyon of another small one which joins it here—and since we had not learned if this one could be negotiated or not—we feared finding ourselves obliged (if we went down and crossed the river) to do the necessary backtracking which on this precipice would be extremely difficult. So as not to have to risk it, we halted above and sent the genízaro Juan Domingo to go across the river and find out if the said canyon had an exit, but if he did not find it this afternoon to return so that we might continue upstream along this side until we found the Indians' ford and trail.

After the latter was dispatched on foot, Lucrecio Muñiz said that if we let him he would also go bareback on a horse, taking along the things needed for making a fire and sending up smoke signals in case

shallow notch about 150 yards long. In their ascent toward the southeast they were actually approaching Lee's Ferry, so that they crested the ridge only about two miles from San Benito Salsipuedes; yet they were 1,700 vertical feet above the Colorado River.

371. Slightly over 11.8 miles.
372. The formation now carries the name Castle Rock.
373. Navajo Creek Canyon.

he found an exit, so that with this message we would try finding our way down and shorten the delay. We told him to go, but reminded him that we expected him back this afternoon, whether he found the exit or not. They did not return, and so we passed the night here without being able to water the horse herds while being so adjacent to the river. We named the place El Vado de los Chamas, or San Carlos.[374] Today two leagues[375] east-southeast.

November 4

On the 4th, day broke without our learning about the two whom we had dispatched yesterday on the reconnaissance mentioned. The meat from the second horse had run out, we had not eaten a thing today, and so we breakfasted on toasted pads of low prickly pear cactus and gruel made from a tiny fruit[376] they brought from the riverbank. This tiny fruit of itself has a good taste but, crushed and boiled in water the way we had it today, is very insipid. On seeing how late it was and that the two aforementioned ones did not show up, we ordered that an attempt be made to get the animal herd down to the river and on the bank to slaughter another horse. They got them down with great difficulty, some of the mounts injuring themselves because, when they lost a foothold on the big rocks, they rolled down a long distance.

A little before nightfall, the genízaro Juan Domingo returned, asserting that he had found no way out and that the other one, leaving the horse midway in the canyon, had kept on following some fresh Indian tracks. And so we decided to continue upstream until we found a good ford and passable terrain on one and the other side.

November 5

On the 5th we left San Carlos, no matter if Lucrecio had failed to return, his brother Andrés remaining behind with orders to wait for him until evening, and for him to try to overtake us tonight. We went along this western side and over many ridges and gullies a league and a half to the north; we went down into a dry arroyo[377] and very high-walled

374. "The Hill of the Chamas," or "Saint Charles." The campsite was on the west rim of the canyon opposite the mouth of Navajo Creek. The site is now covered by Lake Powell.

375. About 5 1/4 miles.

376. Probably hackberries.

377. Warm Creek. At the upper end of the trail out of Warm Creek to the east, researchers found a rock cairn marking the spot.

canyon where there was a great deal of copper sulphate. In it we found a little-used trail; we followed it and by means of it came out of the canyon, passing over a brief shelf of soft [white?] rock, difficult but capable of improvement. We kept on going and, after we went a league and a quarter toward the north-northeast, found water, even though a little, and enough pasturage; and since it was almost dark, we halted close to a high mesa, naming the place Santa Francisca Romana.[378] To-day three short leagues.[379]

Tonight it rained heavily here, and it snowed in some places. It was raining at daybreak and kept it up for some hours. About six in the morning Andrés Muñiz arrived, saying that his brother had not turned up. This news caused us plenty of worry, because he had been three days without provisions and no covering other than his shirt, since he had not even taken trousers along—for, even though he crossed the river on horseback, the horse swam for a long stretch and the water reached almost to the shoulders wherever it faltered. So when the genízaro mentioned decided to go and look for him for this reason, by following the tracks from where he saw him last, we sent him on his way with meat for provision and with orders to leave the mount behind if it could not get out of the canyon and to proceed on foot; and should he find him on the other side, for them to look along it for signs of us and to come after us—and if on this one, to try to overtake us as quickly as possible.

November 6

On the 6th, after it had stopped raining, we left Santa Francisca and headed northeast, and after we had gone three leagues we were stopped for a long time by a strong blizzard and tempest consisting of rain and thick hailstones amid horrendous thunder claps and lightning flashes.[380] We recited the Virgin's Litany, for her to implore some relief for us, and God willed for the tempest to end. We continued east for half a league and halted near the river because it kept on raining and some rock

378. Near the base of Ramona Mesa, near the head of Cottonwood Wash, one of the tributaries of Warm Creek.

379. As they measured only "short leagues," this date they probably made something less than 7.5 miles.

380. They were in Gunsight Canyon, probably on the west bank of that gulch, when the storm broke with all its fury, sending a flash flood down the canyon and causing the party to stop until the storm and flood had cleared.

cliffs blocked our way. We named the place San Vicente Ferrer.[381] Today three leagues and a half.[382]

Don Juan Pedro Cisneros went to see if the ford lay around here and came back to report having seen how very wide the river was hereabouts and that he did not think it was deep according to the current, but that we could get to it only through a nearby canyon. We sent two others to inspect it and to ford the river, and they came back saying that everything was difficult to negotiate. We did not give much credence to the latters' report, and so we decided to examine it ourselves next day along with Don Juan Pedro Cisneros. Before night came the genízaro arrived with the said Lucrecio.

November 7

On the 7th we went out very early to inspect the canyon[383] and ford, taking along the two genízaro, Felipe and Juan Domingo, so that they might ford the river on foot since they were good swimmers. In order to have the mounts led down to the canyon mentioned, it became necessary to cut steps with axes on a stone cliff for the space of three yards or a bit less.[384] Over the rest of it the horse herds were able to get across, although without pack or rider.

We got down to the canyon, and after going a mile we reached the river[385] and went along it downstream for about as far as two musket shots, now through the water, now along the edge, until we came to the widest part of its currents where the ford[386] appeared to be. One man

---

381. The site was within a mile of the Colorado River just southeast of the base of Gunsight Butte on the west side of Padre Creek, but not in sight of either it or the Colorado.

382. Slightly over nine miles.

383. On the west rim of Glen Canyon overlooking the likely fording place.

384. Access to the floor of Padre Creek was over a steep sandstone slope which a man could negotiate without danger. However, lest the horses lose their footing and tumble to the canyon floor, the expedition hacked out some shallow footholds, or steps, for about ten feet in one of the most dangerous places, making it less hazardous for the animals. This used to be one of Utah's most historic sites. It is now covered with 550 feet of water from Lake Powell.

385. That is, the Colorado River. The distance was actually not more than a quarter of a mile.

386. This is located where a permanent sandbar was found at the base of the west canyon wall. Diagonally across from that bar was a similar one on the opposite side of the river. A ripple in the water surface indicated the shallowest point leading directly to

waded in and found it all right, not having to swim at any place. We
followed him on horseback, entering a little farther down, and in its
middle two mounts which went ahead missed bottom and swam
through a short channel. We held back, although with some peril, until
the first one who crossed on foot came back from the other side to lead
us, and we successfully passed over without the horses on which we
were crossing ever having to swim.[387]

We notified the rest of the companions, who had stayed behind at
San Vicente, to hoist with lassos and ropes—down a not very high cliff
to the ford's bend—the equipment, saddles, and other effects and to
bring the horse herd along the route we had come. They did it that way
and finished crossing the river about five in the afternoon, praising
God our Lord and firing off some muskets in demonstration of the
great joy we all felt in having overcome so great a problem, one which
had caused us so much labor and delay—even when the main cause of
our having suffered so much, ever since we entered Parussi country,
was our having no one to guide us through so much difficult terrain.
For through the lack of expert help we made many detours, wasted
time from so many days spent in a very small area, and suffered hunger
and thirst.

And now that we had undergone all this, we got to know the best
and most direct route where the water sources helped in the planning
of average day's marches, and we kept on gathering reports about the
others, especially when we stopped going south the day we left San
Dónulo or Arroyo del Taray[388]—because, from this place, we could
have gone to the bounteous water source that we found on the plain
which came after; from here we could have conveniently reached another copious water source which lies some three leagues northeast of

---

that sandbar. It was evidently from this point that the camp gear was lowered over the
cliff to the sandbar. The journal statement that the ford was a mile wide would have to
mean from Padre Creek to the sandbar at the east side of the river. The water at the
ripple was not more than three feet deep. The actual fording place probably changed
slightly from time to time, depending on the shifting sandbar.

387. This marks the famous "Crossing of the Fathers." Most of the area traversed
by the 1776 Spanish party now lies beneath the waters of Lake Powell. At the point
where the padres crossed, the lake is now about 550 feet deep. Several research teams
explored this region in 1938, 1950, and 1958, prior to the construction of the Glen Canyon Dam. See David E. Miller, "Discovery of Glen Canyon, 1776," *Utah Historical
Quarterly*, 26 (1958): 221–37.

388. That is, October 15, 1776.

San Ángel. From this one to Santa Gertrudis; from here we could have gone three leagues, to halt in the same arroyo having sufficient water and pastures, gain as much distance as possible during the afternoon by heading northeast, and, by following the same direction and entirely avoiding the sierra, arrive next day at El Río de Santa Teresa, three or four leagues north of San Juan Capistrano; from this river to San Diego toward the east-southeast, and from this place to the ford without any special inconvenience while evading many detours, inclines, and bad stretches.

But God doubtless disposed that we obtained no guide, either as merciful chastisement for our faults or so that we could acquire some knowledge of the peoples living hereabouts. May His most holy will be done in all things, and may His holy name be glorified.

The river's ford is very good. Here it must be a little more than a mile wide. Already here the rivers Navajó and Dolores flow joined together,[389] along with the rest which we have said in this diary enter either one or the other; and in all that we saw around here no settlement can be established along their banks, nor can one even go one good day's march downstream or upstream along either side with the hope of their waters being of service to the people and horse herd, because, besides the terrain being bad, the river flows through a very deep gorge. Everything else adjacent to the ford consists of very tall cliffs and precipices. Eight or ten leagues to the northeast of it rises a round mountain, high but small, which the Payuchis—who begin from here onward—call Tucane, meaning Black Mountain,[390] and the only one to be seen hereabouts. The river passes very close to it.

On this eastern side at the ford itself, which we named La Purísima Concepción de la Virgen Santísima,[391] there is a small bend with good pasturage. We spent the night in it and took a bearing of its latitude by the North Star, and it is 36° 55'.[392]

389. The Colorado River.
390. This high but small, round mountain, called Tucane by the Payuchis (Southern Paiute) and *cerro negro* by the padres, is known today as Navajo Mountain.
391. "The Immaculate Conception of the Most Holy Virgin."
392. Here their calculation is too low; they were slightly above 37°, about three miles north of the present Utah-Arizona boundary.

BRIEF ACCOUNT OF THE PEOPLES WHOM, FROM EL VALLE
DEL SEÑOR SAN JOSÉ TO EL VADO DEL RÍO GRANDE DE
COSNINA, INCLUSIVE, WE SAW, HAD DEALINGS WITH, AND
LEARNED ABOUT FROM REPORTS

In this land—which, although we traveled over it for a hundred
long leagues[393] because of the detours we made, must be sixty Spanish
leagues from north to south and forty from east to west[394]—there reside a great number of peoples, all of pleasing appearance, very engag-
ing, and extremely timid. For this last reason, and because all whom we
saw speak the Yuta language in the same manner as the westernmost
Payuchis, we named all these of whom we are now speaking Yutas Cobardes.[395] The name of each comes from the area it inhabits, whereby
they are distinguished according to several provinces or territories—
not according to nations, as all the Yutas known heretofore compose a
single nation, or let us call it kingdom, divided into five provinces
which are the ones known by the common name of Yutas: the Muhuachi Yutas, the Payuchi Yutas, the Tabehuachis, and the Sabuaganas.

So, in the same way, are the Yutas Cobardes divided into Huascaris,
who inhabit El Valle del Señor San José and its vicinity; Parussis, who
come next toward the south and southwest and inhabit the banks and
vicinity of the small Río de Nuestra Señora del Pilar and are the only
ones from among all these we saw who devote themselves to the cul-
tivation of maize; the Yubuincariris, who live almost to the south of the
Parussis and hereabouts are the closest to El Río Grande; the Ytimpa-
bichis, who live on mesas and cliffs standing near El Paraje de Santa
Bárbara toward the north; and the Pagampachis, who likewise inhabit
bad terrain of sterile mesas and embankments, for, although they have
a spacious valley and El Río Grande, as we already said, runs through
it, they cannot avail themselves of the latter's waters for irrigating.

According to the Yubuincariris' account, downstream from them
to the south-southwest there dwell others whom they call Payatammunis. We also learned that to the west and west-northwest of the Huascaris there lived other peoples of the same language as themselves. All
the rest (who are many), who live upstream on this eastern or northern
side all over the sierra which comes down from the Lagunas—and the
country lying between them and the last northern rivers we crossed

393. Something over 263 miles.
394. That is, 157.8 miles by 105.2 miles.
395. Apparently refers to the Southern Paiutes.

before they came together—are, according to the reports we got, of this same kind of Indians and belong partly to the Yutas Barbones, partly to the Huascaris, and partly to the Lagunas, depending on what proximity these are to each other for the greater similarity with which those closest speak the common language.

November 8

On the 8th we left the ford and stopping point of La Concepción and climbed the river's box canyon over a not too troublesome reclining cliff. We headed south-southeast by following a well-beaten path and traveled five leagues over sandy terrain with some gullies. We turned east for a league and halted near the last standing cliff in a chain of them extending from the river up to here,[396] naming the place San Miguel.[397] In it there was good pasturage and plenty of rainwater. Today six leagues.[398]

Today we found many footprints of Indians but did not see any of them. Wild sheep breed hereabouts in such abundance that the tracks look like those of great droves of tame sheep. They are larger than the domestic ones, of the same shape as theirs, but very much swifter. Today we finished the horsemeat we had with us, and so we ordered another one killed. Tonight we were very cold, more so than on the other side.

November 9

On the 9th we lost the trail, could not find a way by which to descend to a nearby canyon to the southeast of us, nor get across more than half a league's length of a mass of cliffs and ridges which prevented us from pursuing our intended route.[399] This is why we headed east-northeast,

396. These are the magnificent cliffs of Tse Tonte. Tse Tonte is prominently visible from Wahweap Marina on Lake Powell or from Page, Arizona. En route the party had passed along the west base of Padre's Butte, thence along the east side of the outstanding "Domínguez Buttes" before crossing westward from Face Canyon drainage into that of Labyrinth Canyon by way of a relatively low and wide pass that separates Tse Tonte from the Domínguez Buttes.

397. It lies in a pocket of large boulders at the south foot of the thousand-foot-high Tse Tonte. One wonders why the padres failed to mention the spectacular setting of this campsite.

398. About 15 3/4 miles.

399. In spite of the journal entry it seems unlikely that Domínguez and Escalante knew, on November 9, that they would have to descend the canyon to the southeast of them. Probably this entry was added at a later date. The only point of descent into the

and, after we had traveled two leagues of bad terrain, the same obstacle forced us to halt atop a mesa,[400] unable to go a step farther.[401] Near this mesa we found some camps of Payuchi Yutas,[402] who border on the Cosninas. We made great efforts through the Laguna and other companions to have them approach where we were, and, either because they suspected that we were friends of the Moquis, with whom they share great enmity, or because they had never seen Spaniards and greatly feared us, we could not get them to come near.

November 10

On the 10th, very early, both of us went to their camps along with the interpreter and the Laguna. We could not get near to where they were, even by coming on foot. We sent over the two mentioned, while we stayed behind on an elevation from which we could see them and were seen by them,[403] so that when they saw us alone they might approach us more freely and with less fear. After the interpreter had cajoled them for more than two hours, five came over and, on approaching us, turned back and fled without our being able to detain them. The interpreter went back again to see if they would sell us some provisions, but they replied that they had none.

They told him that the Cosninas lived very close to here, but that they were now away, wandering through the forests gathering piñon nuts, and that a short distance from here we would find two trails, one toward the Cosninas and another to El Pueblo de Oraibi in Moqui.[404]

---

canyon is not that difficult to find—providing one is looking for it. More likely the party lost the trail in the sands and kept moving eastward in hopes they would find it. They did realize, however, that they were probably rimrocked by the long line of cliffs paralleling their route about half a mile to the south. These cliffs, together with the higher elevations along the edge, make up the "rocks and ridges" referred to.

400. No name was given to this campsite. They camped in a low point on the east side of Weed Bench, which is almost directly east-northeast by compass needle (not true north) from the campsite of San Miguel.

401. As they neared the eastern edge of Weed Bench, they headed for a low point between two mesas but found to their chagrin that the cliff they had been paralleling merely curved to the north and again cut them off. Thus they faced the "same difficulty," being rimrocked overlooking a tributary of West Canyon, and could not take another step forward.

402. About 150 feet below them, however, they could see a temporary encampment of nomadic Paiute Indians.

403. They remained on the canyon rim, that is, on the eastern edge of Weed Bench.

404. A Hopi village located on Third Mesa in Northeastern Arizona. Oraibi is considered by some scholars as the oldest continuously occupied town in the United

They also showed him how to find the trail we had lost, saying that we would have to retrace our steps to San Miguel and from here go down to the canyon mentioned before. And in this we wasted most of the day, and during the rest of it we got back to El Paraje de San Miguel,[405] getting closer by half a league to the arroyo or canyon into which we had not been able to descend before; then we halted where the descent began. Today half a league[406] to the southeast.

November 11

On the 11th, very early, the descent was explored,[407] the lost trail was found, and we continued on our way. We went down into the canyon[408] with little trouble because, even though there are some dangerous stretches and all of it is precipitous, the Indians have fixed it up with loose stones and sticks, and in the last one they have a stairway of the same, more than three yards long and two wide.[409] Here two little streams meet[410] which run into the large one near El Paraje de San Carlos.[411] We climbed up to the opposite side by a precipitous and rocky ridge-cut which lies between the two rivulets, making many turns and

States. It is said that they have been living in this village on this mesa for over 1,000 years. It vies with the Pueblo of Acoma in New Mexico for this distinction.

405. This campsite cannot be pinpointed precisely. Although they must have been near the trail over the edge of the canyon, the journal entry for November 11 says that they had to search for the trail. For protection from the elements they probably camped in one of the shallow gullies above the edge of the deep canyon.

406. That is, 1.32 miles.

407. Only one possible point of descent exists, a relatively narrow, boulder-choked, dugway-type incline that leads about sixty vertical feet down to the more level slickrock. Little evidence of trail work can be detected.

408. Navajo Canyon. In this instance it consists of a network of smaller steep-walled canyons feeding into the main branch. The trail winds through side gulches, around isolated mini-buttes, and across precipitous ledges.

409. It appears that the route through the slickrock canyon and past San Miguel was the main route to and from the "Crossing of the Fathers" until that crossing was virtually replaced by use of the ferryboat at Lee's Ferry in the 1870s. At that time the trail was virtually abandoned. After their movement into the area during the 1860s and 1870s, Navajos used this trail and the Crossing of the Fathers for only a few years. The Navajos did, however, wish to graze their stock on Weed Bench, to which an extension of the trail was built. Although used frequently until 1974, the trail may soon be almost completely abandoned because of the flooding of the trail ford at Navajo Creek by Lake Powell.

410. Navajo Creek and Kaibito Wash.

411. Having reached the floor of the canyon, the padres found themselves at the confluence of Navajo and Kaibito creeks, which today is flooded by the waters of Lake Powell. As the journal states, the explorers climbed out of the canyon over a steep, rocky route between the two streams.

passing some rock shelves which are perilous and improvable only by dint of crowbars.[412] We finished the ascent toward midday, having gone two leagues east-southeast in the descent and ascent.[413]

Here there are two small buttes[414] northeast of the trail. From the smaller one we swung southeast, and after going three leagues over good terrain[415] we halted, even if without water, because there was good pasturage for the horse herds and plenty of firewood to ward off the severe cold we were experiencing—naming the place San Proto.[416] Today five leagues.[417]

November 12

On the 12th we set out from San Proto and headed south-southeast, traveling now on an open course and good terrain for three leagues, and on the same course found a small spring of good water[418] where all the men and the horse herd drank after the ice was broken. According to what the vestiges show, it is a stopping place for the Cosninas when they travel to the Payuchis. We continued south along the same course, feeling extremely cold, and after traveling four leagues of very good country we left the direct route to Moqui, as it had been indicated by the Payuchis, and followed the one more traveled by the Cosninas toward the south-southwest; then, after going one league, we found sev-

412. The trail, which has been little used in recent times, goes up close to the canyon wall of Kaibito Creek. At a point about a quarter of a mile from the canyon floor a substantial amount of work has been done on the trail to get up and/or down through some flinty limestone ledges in order to pass under a cliff immediately above Kaibito Creek. One mile from the canyon floor the trail turns abruptly to the north-northeast and goes up a wide cleft for about half a mile and then swings south-southeast and ascends a very steep slickrock slope for about 150 yards. This is the steepest part of the trail. Since 1776 someone has picked out a series of steps in the rocks at this point.

413. Once over the steep part, the trail continues south-southeast through an open slickrock area for half a mile, the last part of which passes over a moderately steep slope. The trail tops out at a point approximately 800 feet above and three miles from Navajo Creek.

414. Today's "Small Butte" and "Tsai Skizzi Rock."

415. Once out of the canyon the party traveled about eight miles over "good terrain" across Cedar Tree Bench.

416. The campsite was nearly four miles south-southeast of Tsai Skizzi Rock, the most prominent formation in this immediate area.

417. About 13 miles.

418. A tributary of Kaibito Wash located at a point about five miles northeast of Kaibito village.

eral small dwellings or deserted camps and indications that many herds of cattle and horses had been pastured hereabouts for some time. We kept on along the same course, and after we had gone a league and a half southwest, night came and we halted without water, naming the site San Jacinto.[419] Today nine leagues and a half.[420]

Because of the persisting great cold, we held back for a spell while the rest of the companions went on ahead in order to build a fire and warm up Don Bernardo Miera, who was ready to freeze on us and who we feared could not survive so much cold. That is why the rest of the companions arrived ahead of us at the spring mentioned and, before we could overtake them, kept on going without filling up the vessels which we brought along for this purpose. Because of their carelessness we suffered great thirst tonight.

November 13

On the 13th we started out from San Jacinto toward the south-southwest along the course mentioned, and over good terrain of woods and abundant pasturages, and after going two leagues we swung south a league and a half, and among some big rocks we found sufficient water for the men and almost enough for all the horses. We continued south over a sandy plain for two leagues, and half of one to the southeast, and halted about a league beyond another waterhole[421] with bad water which we found on the same route. We named the place El Espino[422] because we caught a porcupine today, and here we tasted flesh of the richest flavor.

We were all so much in need of nourishment now, since we had not eaten anything but a piece of toasted hide the night before, and so the porcupine shared among so many only served to whet the appetite. Hence we ordered another horse deprived of its life. It was something we had not done sooner because we had expected to find provisions in some Cosnina camp, but not even a recent vestige of them had we seen. Today six leagues.[423]

419. On the north edge of a small butte near the center of a valley about four miles east of Preston Mesa.
420. Very close to 25 miles.
421. Standing Rock Well, which is located in a weirdly eroded cluster of sandstone rocks.
422. This campsite was not located near any distinctive topographic feature, but was merely out in a large field of bedrock sandstone and sand dunes. It was on the present road about five miles directly north of Tuba City, Arizona.
423. About 14 3/4 miles.

November 14

On the 14th we left El Espín and headed south-southeast, and after
going a little less than a league we found en route a big waterhole of
good water,⁴²⁴ where the entire horse herd drank to satisfaction. We
kept going southeast, and at three-quarters of a league we entered a
canyon⁴²⁵ where four springs of good water emerge.⁴²⁶ We traveled
southeast through it for half a league and arrived at a small farm and
camp of the Cosninas, all of it pretty and well arranged—the farmland
is irrigated by means of the four springs mentioned and by two other
copious ones which rise next to it;⁴²⁷ here this year the Cosninas
planted maize, squash, watermelon, and muskmelon. By the time we
arrived they had gathered their harvest and, judging from the refuse or
scraps of everything we found, it had been an abundant one, and especially that of beans. For if we had made camp here, we could have
gleaned half a bushel of it. The farmland is surrounded by peach
trees.⁴²⁸

Besides the several huts made of boughs, there was a very well constructed little house of stone and mud. In it were the baskets, jars, and
other utensils of these Indians. These, judging from the tracks, had
gone away some days before, perhaps to look for piñon nuts in the adjacent high sierra toward the south-southwest. Trails went off from the
camp in different directions, and we did not know which one to take to
go to Moqui, for we could no longer go farther afield looking for the
Cosninas, as much from the lack of supplies as from the extreme severity with which winter was plaguing us.

424. Not identified.
425. Pasture Canyon.
426. Today four conspicuous large springs burst from aquifers at ground level or
slightly above in alcoves on the east canyon wall.
427. Other springs in addition to the four already mentioned occur in the vicinity. The combined waters of all these springs irrigate fields which are to be seen at in-
termittent intervals throughout the canyon from its head to Pasture Canyon Reservoir,
a distance of about 2.75 miles. A constant flow of water reaches the reservoir, which
stores water for the irrigated fields of the Hopi village of Moenkopi, two miles farther
downstream and overlooking Moenkopi Wash.
428. With its cornfields and cottonwood trees and hundred-foot-high red sandstone walls, Pasture Canyon is as delightful today as it must have been in 1776. The
canyon, a five-mile-long oasis in the desert, is the only watercourse of its kind in the
area, and it nicely fits the journal description. Although Indian farmers are the main
tillers of the canyon fields today, Lot Smith, early Mormon pioneer settler in the
Moenkopi–Tuba City area in the 1870s, operated a farm just south of the middle section of the canyon.

We took a trail which went southeast, traveled for two leagues over altogether flat country,[429] passing by some springs of good water, and crossed a small river which flows from northeast to southwest and carries as much water as an adequate irrigation ditch.[430] It has its small poplar grove and small meadows with very poor pasturage where we crossed it. Beyond the river we climbed a mesa[431] where there was a small lake and several banked pools of rainwater, and they serve as ponds and watering places for the Moqui cattle which we were already beginning to see in numerous herds. We traveled over the mesa for two and a half leagues to the east-southeast, went up a high hill, and because night was approaching and there was good pasturage for the horse herds, we halted—naming the place Cuesta de los Llanos[432] because from here begin the spreading plains and countryside having no mesas, woods, or sierras, but very good pasturages which extend southeastward far beyond Moqui. Today six leagues and a quarter.[433]

November 15

On the 15th we left La Cuesta de los Llanos, headed east-southeast, and traveled over the plains for nine leagues without finding water during the whole day's march, so as not to go astray looking for it. We found it in a narrow valley where there was a great deal of sagebrush of the kind they call *chico*. We halted in it, naming it La Cañada de los Chicos.[434] Today nine leagues[435] to the southwest.

We no longer had a thing for eating supper tonight because the horsemeat on hand was not enough for all. There were large cattle-herds hereabouts, and all the companions wanted to kill a cow or a heifer. They kept impatiently insisting that we should let them relieve

429. They left Pasture Canyon and headed southeast across open desert. They may have continued to the vicinity of the present reservoir before leaving the canyon, but it seems clear that they did not reach the present site of Moenkopi. The present village, an offshoot of the Hopi town of Oraibi, was not established until the mid-1870s.

430. Moenkopi Wash.

431. Coal Mesa, on the Moenkopi Plateau.

432. This camp was near the head of the spectacular Coal Mine Canyon and very close to Arizona State Highway 264.

433. That is, 16.44 miles.

434. Located at or near the right bank of Dinnebito Wash.

435. The distance covered this date was under 7 leagues, about 18 miles, not 9 leagues, a difference of about 6 miles.

the need from which we all were suffering by this means. Realizing that we were already near El Pueblo de Oraibi, that this would cause some trouble between us and the Moqui people and defeat our purpose— which was to exert anew our efforts in behalf of the Light, and meekness of the Gospel, as against their willful blindness and inveterate obstinacy[436]—we ordered another horse to be killed, and that no one was to approach those herds even if, as they assured us, they were runaways or public property.

November 16

On the 16th we set out from La Cañada de los Chicos toward the east-southeast, went three leagues, and near a high mesa turned east-north-east for a quarter of a league. Here we found a well-beaten trail and concluded that it went to one of the Moqui pueblos. We followed it and, after going three leagues northeast over good and altogether flat country, and a little less than two north, we arrived at the mesa of El Pueblo de Oraibi. We ordered the companions to halt at the mesa's foot, that none except those going up with us should approach the pueblo until we gave the word.[437]

We went up without incident. As we started to enter the pueblo a large number of Indians, big and small, surrounded us. We kept asking for the ritual headman and war captains in a language they did not know, and as we tried to go over to the ritual headman's house they stopped us and one of them told us in Navajo not to enter the pueblo.[438] Don Juan Pedro Cisneros then asked him spiritedly in the same language whether or not they were friends of ours. This quieted them down, and a very old man led us to his home and lodged us in it,

436. Throughout the Spanish colonial period the Hopi were referred to as the "obstinate Hopi" for their steadfast refusal to accept Christianity.

437. At Old Oraibi, Father Vélez de Escalante was on familiar ground. During June and July 1775 he had traveled to the Hopi villages from Zuñi to obtain geographical information and to learn about the Hopi and their customs as a means of propagating the faith. His diary of that trip, which contains many more details about the Hopi than in this 1776 account, has been translated and edited by Eleanor Adams in "Fray Silvestre and the Obstinate Hopi," *New Mexico Historical Review* 38 (April 1963): 97–138.

438. For the past several years the pueblo of Old Oraibi has been closed to white visitors. A handpainted sign, posted at the entrance of the village, reads: "WARNING: No outside white visitors allowed. Because of your failure to obey the laws of our tribe as well as the laws of your own, this village is hereby closed."

offering us a room in which to spend the night, and their customary victuals. Today seven leagues.[439]

Tonight the ritual headman with two very old men came to visit us, and, after having let us know that they were our friends, offered to sell us the provisions we might need. We let them know that we much appreciated it.

439. The total mileage for the day is given as seven leagues (almost 18.5 miles), although the several distances listed in the journal for that day add up to about eight leagues. Seven leagues is the more accurate figure, however.

✠

ORAIBI—SANTA FE
NOVEMBER 17–JANUARY 3

November 17

On the 17th, quite early, they brought us at our lodging some baskets or trays of flour, beef tallow, maize paperbread,[440] and other kinds of food supplies. We promptly purchased what we could, since of what we most needed they brought the least. For lack of an interpreter, we were unable to discuss their civil submission as it was opportune and as we desired it. We made them understand some things, especially the ritual headman and our host and benefactor; they listened attentively, but let us know little else than that they wished to preserve their friendship with the Spaniards. The ritual headman told us that he had already notified the rest of the pueblos to give us shelter and to sell us the provisions necessary for reaching Zuni.

We let them know that we were very grateful for this favor and the other ones we had received from them, and after midday we left Oraibi for El Pueblo de Shongopavi;[441] and, after going nearly two leagues and a quarter southeast, we arrived when the sun had already set, and they welcomed us attentively, promptly giving us lodging. Today two leagues and a quarter[442] southeast.

November 18

On the 18th, when the Indian councilmen of this pueblo had assembled, along with those of the adjacent ones, Shipaulovi and Mo-

---

440. A paper-thin bread made from fine cornflour; it tastes like cornflakes and is really the forerunner of cornflakes. It is delicious. To learn how it is made see *Me and Mine: "The Life Story of Helen Sekaquaptewa* (Tucson: University of Arizona Press, 1969), 112–15.

441. The Hopi village located on the southern tip of Second Mesa.

442. Almost six miles. The journal description of this day's travel nicely illustrates a common feature of the diary. The actual direction of travel was first nearly east and then nearly south. The destination of Shongopavi is southeast of Old Oraibi. Thus, the "two and a quarter leagues to the southeast" is quite correct.

shongnovi,[443] after we had tendered them our thanks—partly by signs and partly in Navajo—for the courtesies and good reception they had given us, we preached to them; and they replied that they could not parley with us for their being unable to understand Castilian, or ourselves the Moqui language, that we should go over to Walpi,[444] where there were some who knew the Castilian tongue, and that there, by talking all that we wanted with the ritual headmen and war captains, we would learn about what they all desired.

But when we insisted that, in case they had understood us, they should answer for their own selves, they further replied that the ritual headman and war captain of Oraibi had sent them word to welcome us, to take care of us and sell us provisions, while cultivating our friendship without treating about or admitting any other matter—in short, that they wanted to be our friends but not Christians. This over, we gave the Indian who had lodged us and treated us so well a woolen blanket for his wife, figuring that in this way they would better appreciate our gratitude and would become more fond of us; but it did not turn out the way we expected because, when the Indian woman gladly took it, a brother of hers snatched it away from her and threw it at us with a mean look on his face.

We presumed that his suspicious mind imagined in this innocent act of recompense some perverse motive contrary to our honor and profession, and so we tried to make him understand the true intention with the seriousness and prudence which the case called for. Then the Indian, wanting to make up for the wrong he had done us—although his fault was not as grave as it appeared—put us in another predicament which was even greater than the first as he addressed us a long time without our understanding what he was saying, pointing at Padre Fray Silvestre and Don Juan Pedro Cisneros.

After having made us ponder a great deal, and those who had assembled having left, he said in Navajo that he had learned about what took place in Oraibi when the said Padre Fray Silvestre and Don Juan Pedro had been there the summer of the year before,[445] and that he had been present in Walpi when the Cosnina man spoke to Padre Fray Sil-

443. These are the two other Hopi villages located on Second Mesa.
444. A Hopi village located on First Mesa along with Hano, a Tewa village, and Sichomovi.
445. See Eleanor Adams's translation of this visit, cited in footnote 437, above.

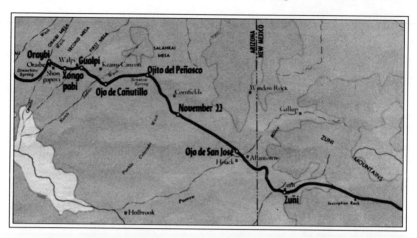

ORAIBI TO SANTA FE, NOVEMBER 17–JANUARY 3

vestre and informed him about the route from Moqui to the Cosninas, and that now we had followed the same trail—that he was not allowing his brother-in-law and sister to accept the blanket because if they took it their relatives and neighbors would be angry with them.

He said this to placate us, but we could not draw out of him with any clarity whatever else he wanted to or had wanted to tell us concerning the matter, although it is not too difficult to infer it from the events which had occurred [the year] before.

In the afternoon we left for Walpi and, after going east two leagues and more than a quarter, we arrived when it was already dark. Our small party remained at the foot of the cliff, and we went up with some of them. The Tanos and Walpis very joyfully received us, and they lodged us in the home of the Tanos' ritual headman, where we spent the night. Today two leagues and a quarter.[446]

After we had rested a short while, a backslider Indian named Pedro from El Pueblo de Galisteo[447] in New Mexico, already very old and enjoying much authority in this one of the Tanos in Moqui, informed us that they were currently engaged in a cruel war with the Navajo

446. Nearly six miles.
447. Located about 25 miles south of Santa Fe. Settled by Tano Indians, its population in 1749 was 350, but smallpox and Comanche raids reduced them so greatly that in 1794 the few survivors moved to Santo Domingo pueblo.

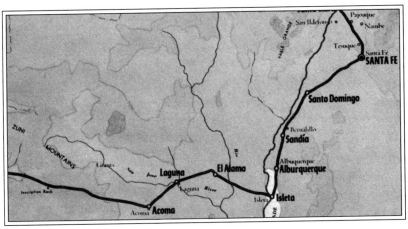

ORAIBI TO SANTA FE, NOVEMBER 17–JANUARY 3

Apaches,[448] and that these had killed and captured many of their people. For this reason, he added, they were wishing for the arrival of some padres and Spaniards, through whom they might beg the lord governor for some aid or defense against these foes. And so they had been particularly delighted when they learned that we had come to visit them, because they hoped that we would bring them support and relief.

This looked to us like one of the finest opportunities for inducing them to submit themselves to the faith and the realms of his majesty (whom God keep). We answered them by giving them great hopes and telling them to summon the councilmen of the other three pueblos to these ones of Walpi, and for all of them to assemble next day in this one of the Tanos in order to discuss this business seriously and at length. Then the Pedro referred to said that he wanted to go over to Santa Fe, if we would take him along with us, in order to arrange with the lord governor, in behalf of the Moquis and Tanos, the alliance which they desired and to request the support which they needed.

We answered him by saying that we would most gladly take him along and would use our good offices with the lord governor in behalf of all the Moquis, but that for this it was necessary that each of the six

448. See Frank D. Reeve, "Early Navaho Geography," *New Mexico Historical Review* 31 (October 1956): 298–306, for a discussion of the Navajo-Apache and their homeland.

pueblos dispatch someone in authority before his lordship's presence. They agreed to come together the next day in the manner suggested, and to summon us when they were already assembled in the under- ground ceremonial chamber[449] to talk over and discuss it all, and to decide on what was best.

November 19

On the 19th the councilmen of Moshongnovi came, and when they were already assembled with the ritual headmen and war captains of these pueblos of the mesa of Walpi inside a ceremonial chamber of the Tanos, the said apostate Pedro conducted us to it, giving us for an in- terpreter another apostate Indian from El Pueblo de Santa Clara named Antonio the Twin, because the latter speaks and understands Castilian well; he kept translating our words into Tewa,[450] and the said Pedro into Moqui, so that all of us in the meeting could understand one another. They related everything that they had discussed before we arrived at the chamber, and that they had agreed on having the apos- tate Pedro go over to La Villa de Santa Fe in our company, in order to request aid from the lord governor in the name of all against the Na- vajo Apaches and establish friendship with the Spaniards—and they begged us to do everything possible in their behalf.

We answered them by saying that we would be on their side in ev- erything, because we loved them as one does his children, and that we very much sympathized with their troubles, but, since God alone is the one who can do everything and governs all, that they could not rid themselves of their sufferings so long as they persisted in their infidelity and did not cease offending Him. We went on expounding to them the gravity of eternal punishments, that if they failed to submit to the Christian religion they would have to suffer without letup in hell—we taking advantage of the afflictions which they had just brought up for greater clarity and force.

We also told them that if they submitted they would enjoy con-

449. These semisubterranean ceremonial chambers of the Hopi (and Zuni) are called Kivas. The Spaniards called them "estufas," as they resembled hot stoves or sweat-houses to them.
450. Tewa is a dialect of the Tanoan language. Tewa is spoken by the New Mexico pueblos of San Juan, Santa Clara, San Ildefonso, Nambe, Tesuque, and the Tewa Indi- ans in the Hopi village of Hano on First Mesa. During the Pueblo Rebellion of 1860 some Tewa speakers from the Rio Grande valley fled to Hopiland and sought refuge and safety on their mesas. They have retained their separate language to this day.

tinual and sure recourse to Spanish arms against all infidels who should war against them, as did the rest of the Christian pueblos of New Mexico, at the same time making them see the futility and inconstancy of the friendships and alliances which they time and again compacted with the Yutas and Navajos. Then, after having told them everything we thought effective and to the point, we told them to declare their decision to us with the understanding that, whether or not it accorded with our desire, we still intended to take their delegates to Santa Fe and assist them in every way possible.

Three times did we make our plea, exhorting them to submit themselves to the Church's bosom by impugning and demonstrating as vain and false the reasons they gave for their not converting to the faith. The first time, they replied that they already knew how the governors sent the padres so that he could bring them under his rule, but that they never had wanted it then or now. In the second, they let us know that, since there were many more gentile nations than there were Christian folk, they wanted to be on the more numerous side, and that, besides this, they lived in country too inconvenient for the services which, as converts, they would have to render the Spaniards.

The plausibility of each one of these arguments having been undone, and now unable to refute, all those in the assembly spoke by turns for a long while, starting with those of higher authority down the line in this wise; and although each one had his say, he expressed himself in dialogue form and concluded his discourse by asking several questions of the others, each one answering by either assenting or denying according to the nature of the questions. In these discourses they recalled the traditions of their forebears and urged their observance, concluding that it was better for them to undergo their present calamities and hardships than to go against them; and they replied that they solely desired our friendship but by no means to become Christians, because the ancient ones had told them and counseled them never to subject themselves to the Spaniards.

We tried to make them see the foolish impiety of such traditions and counsels, but with no success whatsoever. Then, at the very last, they decided that the Pedro mentioned should not go over to La Villa de Santa Fe, he himself disclosing the reason to us when he said: "They no longer want me to go and see the governor because, since I am baptized, they say he will not let me return to Moqui." He feared this much more than the others, and so we were unable to get him to carry out his original intent.

The meeting closed, and we withdrew quite crestfallen back to our lodgings after seeing how invincible was the obstinacy of these unfortunate Indians. And so we decided to go on to Zuni the following day before the passes and trails closed up entirely, for it kept snowing all along. Because of this we were unable to take the polar latitude in which these Moqui pueblos are.

November 20

On the 20th in the afternoon we set out from the pueblos of Walpi and, after going four leagues east by southeast, stopped to spend the night at the water source called El Ojo del Cañutillo, or Ojo de Moqui.[451] Today four leagues.[452]

November 21

On the 21st we left El Ojo del Cañutillo toward the northeast and, after going three leagues, two southeast, then going another two a little more to the east, we halted more than half a league this side of the little water source called El Estiladero, or Ojito del Peñasco.[453] Today seven leagues.[454]

451. From approximately the present site of Polacca, at the base of First Mesa, they rode east by southeast for about 10.5 miles. Actually their trail lay almost directly up Keams Canyon Wash to the east, generally paralleling Arizona State Highway 264, then slightly southeast to the present site of Keams Canyon Village. That Keams Canyon is indeed the Spaniards' "Ojo del Cañutillo" is based on substantial evidence. The location of the spring fits as a matter of distance and direction. Keams Canyon contains the most abundant spring in the area and would correspond with the journal's description in 1775 of Ojo del Cañutillo as "good and sufficient for many people and horses." Some speculation has been aired that the spring visited was Talahogan Spring or perhaps Awatobi Spring, both located about the right distance southeast of Polacca. These latter two springs, however, are small water seeps (*chupaderos*) located high on the sides of the mesa. Further proof is shown by Escalante's 1775 diary entry to the effect that they returned to Zuni from Hopi by a different route, which led him not to Ojo del Cañutillo, but to Awatobi Spring.

452. Ten and a half miles.

453. From their Keams Canyon campsite they followed the natural trail up the canyon to the northeast, passing the future (1863) Kit Carson inscription and the large spring where Thomas Keam established his first trading post in 1875. At a point near the present Twin Dams they left the canyon to the east, then turned again to the northeast to head the three branches of Jeddito Wash. At a point about three miles from the canyon they turned east and continued in this direction for another four miles. Upon heading the wash they turned southeast, then south-southeast for a total of five miles. Camp was made on or near Beshbito Wash about a mile and a half north of present Arizona State Highway 264. It should be noted that the directions southeast, then east to camp, are given in reverse order. To have followed the journal directions explicitly

November 22

On the 22nd we left the companions with what was left of the horse herds, which by now were more worn out, so that they might follow little by little up to Zuni; and we ourselves, along with three of them, took off with dispatch. Then, after having going nine leagues east by southeast, we arrived at the place called Cumaá.[455] Here we rested a bit and continued east for two more leagues. The mounts gave out on us and we had to stop. Today eleven leagues.[456]

November 23

On the 23rd we kept on going, although it snowed all day in most troublesome blizzards, and after traveling on the gallop for twelve leagues, we halted at the place called Kianaituna, or Ojo del Señor San José.[457] Tonight we suffered extreme cold. Today twelve leagues,[458] almost all to the east.

November 24

On the 24th, as soon as it was daylight, we set out from El Ojo del Señor San José toward the southeast, and after going two leagues we stopped awhile to build a fire to warm ourselves, for it was so cold that we feared we could end up frozen in the narrow valley. We continued

---

would have placed their route directly across rugged upper canyons of Jeddito Wash. Since their earlier travel to the northeast was obviously made to avoid Jeddito Wash, it must be concluded that the directions actually traveled were east, then south-southeast to camp. The small water source called El Estiladero or Ojito del Penasco cannot be identified today. It may possibly be Steamboat Spring, located one mile north of Steamboat Trading Post.

454. Almost 18.5 miles.

455. Today known as Sunrise Springs. This important watering point is located on Pueblo Colorado Wash.

456. Close to 29 miles.

457. Pine Springs today. It is located about nine miles west-northwest of the Rio Puerco. Escalante gave a more complete description of this spring in his diary of his June–July 1775 visit to Hopiland.

458. Over 31 miles. A day's gallop of twelve leagues would have been most difficult, for the route lay over hill country covered with piñon-juniper forest and dissected by numerous ravines and gullies that cut directly across the trail. The most substantial of these gullies is Wide Ruin Wash, which the expedition reached at Klagetoh, about ten miles east-southeast of their last camp. From Klagetoh the trail went down Wide Ruin Wash about three miles, then headed up a hill to the east for another three miles. From there it was another twelve miles more southeast to Pine Springs (Kianaituna, or Ojo del Señor San José).

southeast for more than three leagues, and after going two more east by northeast we stopped to change mounts at a water source which the Zunis call Okiappa.[459] We kept on and, having gone three leagues southeast, we arrived extremely exhausted when it was already dark at the pueblo and mission of Nuestra Señora de Guadalupe de Zuni.[460] Today twelve leagues.[461]

November 26

Then, finding ourselves without energy to proceed without delay to La Villa de Santa Fe, we sent notice to the lord governor[462] of our happy arrival at the mission and a brief relation of what is contained in this diary. On the 26th in the afternoon the rest of the companions arrived.

December 13

Because of various events we stayed in this mission until the 13th of December,[463] when we left for La Villa de Santa Fe. And after having

459. Located on the south rim of Whitewater Arroyo, perhaps in a tributary about two or three miles east of the Arizona–New Mexico border and about the same distance north of the present Zuni Reservation.

460. This was Fray Silvestre Vélez de Escalante's assigned mission. He was stationed here in June 1776, when he was ordered by Father Domínguez to report to him in Santa Fe to discuss prospects for an overland trip to Monterey, California. Thus, arriving here was like reaching home after a long, arduous four-month journey.

461. About 31.5 miles.

462. Governor Pedro Fermín de Mendinueta.

463. It has been conjectured that Fathers Domínguez and Vélez de Escalante remained in Zuni for almost three weeks (November 24 to December 13), primarily to rest and to put the finishing touches on their journal. It is also quite possible that they were waiting to participate in the Feast of Our Lady of Guadalupe, which takes place on December 12. As Our Lady of Guadalupe is the patron Saint of the Zuni Mission, this feast was the biggest Christian ceremony of the year. (They may also have wished to observe the great Indian ceremony of Shalako, which occurs in early December each year.) Since Father Vélez de Escalante was still technically assigned to this mission as one of its two ministers (the other being Fray José Mariano Rosete y Peralta), he would have been expected to assist and participate in the preparations for the celebration. Father Domínguez also had duties to perform at Zuni. As official "canonical visitor," he was required to inspect and to report on all the New Mexico missions. In his report he wrote that his visitation of the Zuni Mission was made on December 9, 1776. This report of this inspection, as well as of the other missions, was discovered in 1927 in the Biblioteca Nacional in Mexico City by Professor France V. Scholes. It was translated and edited by Eleanor B. Adams and Fray Angelico Chavez and published in 1956 as *The Missions of New Mexico: A Description by Fray Francisco Atanasio Domínguez*. It is a gold mine of information about life and society in eighteenth-century New Mexico. It was filed away in Mexico with a sarcastic notation in the margin which stated: "This

traveled thirty leagues,[464] we arrived at the mission of San Estéban de Ácoma[465] on the 16th day of the same December.

December 16

Then there fell a snow heavy enough to keep us from hurrying ahead as we had wished.

December 20

On the 20th we left Ácoma for the mission of El Señor San José de la Laguna,[466] where we arrived after traveling four leagues north. Today four leagues.[467]

---

report is intended in part to be a description of New Mexico, but its phraseology is obscure, it lacks proportion, and offers little to the discriminating taste." It is recognized today as one of the most significant and important documents in New Mexico history.

In a letter to his religious superior Fray Isidro Murillo, written from Zuni on November 25, 1776, Father Domínguez states that the provincial will be able to learn more concerning the expedition just completed "in the Diary which I will remit in due course." This is additional evidence of the superior position Father Domínguez held on the expedition.

464. This is almost 79 miles. It took them four days to cover this distance from Zuni to Acoma. On December 13 they probably traveled the well-established trail from Zuni to El Morro, where they spent the night sheltered from the wind by the high cliffs of El Morro. (El Morro is now a National Monument, also called "Inscription Rock.") Travelers from Oñate in 1605 to modern-day Kilroys have left carved inscriptions on this famous rock. There was no Domínguez-Escalante inscription carved, probably due to the cold and the deep snow around the base of the rock. The next day they journeyed the 18.5 miles from El Morro to San Rafael (modern Grants, New Mexico). On the 15th they went to El Nacimiento (McCartys), and on December 16 they reached the Peñol of Acoma, where they remained four days.

465. The Sky City, located on 357-foot mesa. First described by Hernando de Alvarado, a lieutenant of Coronado, in 1540. He said he "found a rock with a village on top, the strongest position that ever was seen in the world, which was called Acuco in their language." The Acoma people have been living on this "Gibraltar of the Desert" for over a thousand years. The mission church of San Estéban Rey, one of the largest churches in America, dates back to Fray Juan Ramírez in 1629. Father Domínguez conducted his inspection of this mission and pueblo during their four-day stay here.

466. The Laguna mission was also inspected by Domínguez at this time. See *The Missions of New Mexico, 1776* for his exact description of this as well as all other New Mexico missions.

467. Ten and a half miles.

December 22

On the 22nd we left La Laguna, and after going six leagues east we halted at the site called El Álamo.[468] Today six leagues.[469]

December 23

On the 23rd we set out from here, and after going five leagues east and four east-southeast we arrived at the mission of San Agustín de la Isleta.[470] Today nine leagues.[471]

December 28

On the 28th we left El Pueblo de la Isleta, and after going four leagues we arrived at the mission of San Francisco Xavier de Alburquerque.[472] Today four leagues.[473]

December 30

On the 30th we set out from here, and after going another four leagues we came to the mission of Nuestra Señora de los Dolores de Sandía.[474] Today four leagues.[475]

468. Now known as Sheep Springs. Located at the intersection of Interstate 40 and New Mexico State Highway 6, some 16 miles east-southeast of Laguna Pueblo.

469. That is, 15.78 miles.

470. Located some 13 miles south of present Albuquerque, New Mexico, on the Rio Grande.

471. About 23.5 miles.

472. The Alburquerque visited by Domínguez and Vélez de Escalante was centered about a plaza now designated as "Old Town," which was much closer to the Rio Grande than the heart of the modern city which has developed to the east. En route to Alburquerque from Isleta the party passed through a heavily populated area, including the settlements of Las Padillas, Pajarito, Armijo, and Atrisco. Note that Alburquerque used to include an extra *r*. The town was named after the Duque de Alburquerque in its founding in 1707. The first *r* was dropped from its spelling shortly after the American takeover of New Mexico in 1846.

473. Ten and a half miles.

474. Located 13 miles north of Albuquerque. The church in Sandia Pueblo is dedicated to San Antonio de Padua rather than Nuestra Señora de los Dolores. At one time both names were used—San Antonio applying to the mission for the Indians and Dolores to the same mission as used by white settlers. In about 1825 the mission of Our Lady of Sorrows was transferred to the nearby Hispano town of Bernalillo. The description of the church in Dominguez' *Missions of 1776* states that the church is unusable, with no roof and in deplorable condition. It saddened his soul to see the marks of the barbarities perpetrated there.

475. The distance is actually closer to five leagues rather than four leagues, or closer to 13 miles than 10.5.

December 31

On the 31st we kept on going, and after traveling seven leagues we arrived at the mission of Nuestro Padre Santo Domingo.[476] Today seven leagues.[477]

January 2, 1777

On the 2nd of January of this year of '77 we reached La Villa de Santa Fe,[478] after having set out from the mission just mentioned.

January 3

On the 3rd of January we presented this diary,[479] the painted token of the Lagunas which received mention therein, and the Laguna Indian. And because everything contained in this diary is true and faithful to what occurred and was observed during our journey, we do sign it on this same 3rd day of January of the year 1777.

Fray Francisco Atanasio Domínguez[480]
Fray Silvestre Vélez de Escalante

476. Santo Domingo was the ecclesiastical capital of New Mexico during the Spanish colonial period. The Commissary of the Franciscans selected Santo Domingo as their headquarters so as to keep it separate from civil and military influence in Santa Fe.

477. Almost 18.5 miles.

478. The circle was completed. They had been gone from Santa Fe for 159 days. They had traveled over 1,700 miles.

479. The original diary submitted on this date has not been located. Several days after its submission it was borrowed back by Father Domínguez so as to allow his secretary, Fray José Palacio, to make a copy. It is from this copy that this translation has been made.

480. The two padres signed the journal on January 3, 1777, with Fray Francisco Atanasio Domínguez signing *first*, that is, above the signature of Fray Silvestre Vélez de Escalante.

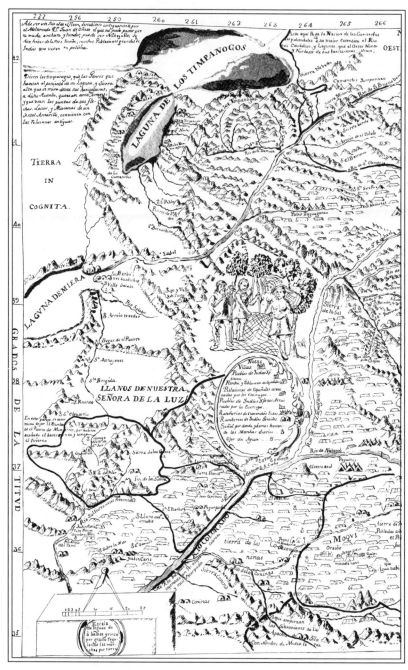

MAP OF DOMÍNGUEZ-ESCALANTE EXPEDITION BY

DON BERNARDO DE MIERA Y PACHECO, 1778

✠

GLOSSARY

Indian tribes

Name in journal	Modern name
Ancamuchis	Cosnina (Havasupai)
Cocomaricopa	Cocomaricopa
Comanches	Comanche
Cosnina	Havasupai
Crusados	Yavapai
Huascaris	Cedar Indians
Jomajaba (Jamajobs)	Mojave
Lagunas	Uintahs
Mescalero Apache	Mescalero Apache
Moqui	Hopi
Navajo Apache	Navajo and/or Apache
Nuhuachi	Mowatei
Pagampachi (Pagampabichis)	Kaibab Indians
Parussi (Parusis)	Shivwits
Payatanumis (Payatammunis)	Unknown
Payuchi Yutas	Southern Paiute
Sabuagana Yutas (Sabuagari)	Mowataviwatsiu
Tabehuachi Yutas	Taviwatsiu
Timpanogotzis	Tompanowotsnunts
Tirangapui	Unknown
Yamparica Comanches	Comanches
Ytimpabichi	Timpeabits
Yubuincarini (Yubuincariris)	Uinkarits
Yutas	Utes
Yutas Ancapagari	Uncompahgre Ute
Yutas Barbones	Bearded Utes (Southern Paiute)
Yutas Chemehuevis	Chevehuevi
Yutas Cobardes	Timid Utes (Southern Paiute)

Rivers and streams

Name in journal	*Modern name*
Aguas Calientes, El Río de	Spanish Fork River, Utah
Ánimas, El Río de las	Animas River
Canjilón, Arroyo del	Canjilon River
Cebolla, El Río de	Cebolla River
Chama, El Río de	Chama River
Cosninas, El Río Grande de	Colorado River
Florido, El Río	Florida River
Grande, El Río	Colorado River or the Rio Grande
Guia, La Fuente de la	Cottonwood Creek
Napestle, El Río de	Arkansas River
Navajó, El Río de	San Juan River
Nuestra Señora de Dolores, El Río de	Dolores River
Nutrias, El Río de las	Nutrias River
Paralíticas, El Río de las	Disappointment Creek
Pilar, El Río del	Kanarra Creek, then Ash Creek
Pinos, Río de Los	Pine River
Plata, El Río de la	The La Plata River
San Andrés, El Río de	Peeteetneet Creek
San Antonio de Padua, El Río de	Provo River
San Bernardo, El Río de	Dolores River
San Buenaventura, El Río de	Green River
San Clemente, El Río de	White River
San Cosme, El Río de	Duchesne River
San Damián, El Río de	Uintah River
San Francisco, El Río de	Uncompahgre River
San Francisco Xavier, El Río de	Gunnison River
San Joaquín, El Río de	The La Plata River
San Juan, El Río de	San Juan River
San Lázaro, El Río de	Mancos River
San Lino, El Río de	Diamond Creek
San Nicolás, El Río de	Hobble Creek or Dry Creek
San Pedro, El Río de	San Miguel River
San Rafael, El Río de	Colorado River
San Simón, El Río de	Brush Creek

San Tadeo, El Río de	Ashley Creek
San Xavier, El Río de	Gunnison River
Santa Ana, El Río de	American Fork River
Santa Catarina de Sena, El Río de	Strawberry River
Santa Gertrudis, El Arroyo de	Bull Rush Wash
Santa Isabel, El Río de	Sevier River
Santa María, El Río de	North Fork of the Gunnison River
Santa Rosa, El Río de	Leroux Creek
Santa Rosalía, El Río de	Jerry Gulch
Santa Teresa, El Río de	Paria River
Señor San José, El Río de	Coal Creek
Sulfúreo, El Río de	Virgin River
Tejedor, El Río de	Beaver River
Tizón, El Río de	Colorado River

Geographical features

Name in journal	*Modern name*
Almagre, El	
Cañón Pintado, El	Painted Canyon
Cerrillo, El	Pahvant Butte
Cerro del Pedernal, El	Flint Hill
Cobre, El	
Cuesta del Susto	Shook hill
Datil, El	
Piedra Parada, El	Chimney Rock
Sierra Blanca de los Timpanois, El	Mount Timpanogos
Sierra de Abajo, El	
Sierra de la Grulla, La	Rocky Mountains
Sierra de la Plata, La	The La Plata Mountains
Sierra de la Sal, La	La Sal Mountains
Sierra de los Sabuaganas	
Sierra de los Tabehuachis	Uncompahgre Plateau
Sierra del Venado Alazán	
Valle de Nuestra Señora de la Merced de los Timpanocuitzis	Utah Valley
Valle de la Piedra Alumbre	Piedralumbre
Valle de Señor San José, El	Cedar Valley, Utah

BIBLIOGRAPHY

Primary Sources
Manuscript materials

Domínguez, Francisco Atanasio, and Vélez de Escalante, Silvestre. Diario y derrotero de los R.R.P.P. Fray Francisco Atanasio Domínguez y Fray Silvestre Vélez de Escalante, para descubrir el camino desde el Presidio de Santa Fe del Nuevo Mexico, al de Monterey, en la California Septentrional.

The original journal maintained on the expedition has not yet been found. It was submitted to the governor of New Mexico on January 3, 1777, by Fray Francisco Atanasio Domínguez but is now apparently lost. Several days after it was submitted to the governor, it was borrowed back for a time by Father Domínguez and a copy was prepared by Fray José Palacio, secretary to Domínguez. This copy is now located in the Ayer Collection in the Newberry Library, Chicago, Illinois. It came from the Mexican Ramírez Collection which consisted of much rifled material from El Convento Grande de San Francisco de Mexico, headquarters of the Franciscan Holy Gospel Province.

Another early manuscript copy is in the Archivo General de Indias (AGI), Seville, Spain. It is in the section Audiencia Guadalajara, 514. This bears the date of July 26, 1777, six months after the return of the expedition.

The Archivo General de Nación (AGN), Mexico City, also has two manuscript copies of the journal. One is in AGN, Historia 26, and was copied on December 27, 1792. The other is in AGN, Historia 62, and was copied in Chihuahua on June 22, 1797.

Other manuscript copies of the journal are in the Biblioteca del Palacio, Madrid; Biblioteca del Ministerio de Asuntos Exteriores, Madrid; Biblioteca de la Real Academia de la Historia, Madrid; the British Museum, London; the Bibliothèque Nationale, Paris; and the Library of Congress, Washington, D.C. These are presumably later copies of copies of the journal.

Printed documents

"Diario y derrotero de los RR. PP. Fr. Francisco Atanasio Domínguez y Fr. Silvestre Vélez de Escalante, para descubrir el camino desde el Presidio de Santa Fe del Nuevo-Mexico, al de Monterey, en la California Septentrional." In *Documentos para la historia de Mexico*, Segunda serie, Tomo I, Mexico, 1854, pp. 375–558. This is the first published version of the journal in Spanish. It is not an accurate rendition of the copies in the Archivo General de Nación, Mexico, or of the Ayer Collection copy in the Newberry Library, Chicago.

Secondary materials
Books, articles, monographs, reports

Adams, Eleanor B. "Fray Silvestre and the Obstinate Hopi." *New Mexico Historical Review* 38 (1963): 97–138. Contains a translation of his journal of the expedition to the Hopi in 1775.

———, ed. "Letter to the Missionaries of New Mexico." *New Mexico Historical Review* 40 (1965): 319–35. Includes "Writings of Fray Silvestre Vélez de Escalante," 333–35.

———, "Fray Francisco Atanasio Domínguez and Fray Silvestre Vélez de Escalante." *Utah Historical Quarterly* 44 (1976): 40–58.

Adams, Eleanor B., and Chavez, Fray Angelico, eds. and trans. *The Missions of New Mexico, 1776: A Description by Fray Francisco Atanasio Domínguez with other contemporary documents.* Albuquerque: University of New Mexico Press, 1956.

Architects/Planners Alliance. *Domínguez-Escalante Trail Bicentennial Interpretive Master Plan and Final Report.* Prepared for The Dominguez-Escalante State/Federal Bicentennial Commission, Salt Lake City, Utah, 1976.

Auerbach, Herbert S. "Father Escalante's Itinerary." *Utah Historical Quarterly* 9 (1941): 109–28.

———, *Father Escalante's Journal, 1776–77: Newly Translated with Related Documents and Original Maps.* Salt Lake City: Utah State Historical Society, 1943. The notes and maps which accompany this work are especially useful.

———, "Father Escalante's Route (as depicted by the Map of Bernardo de Miera y Pacheco)." *Utah Historical Quarterly* 9 (1941): 73–80.

Bolton, Herbert E. "Escalante in Dixie and the Arizona Strip." *New Mexico Historical Review* 3 (1928): 41–72.

———, "Escalante Strikes for California." In *Bolton and the Spanish Borderlands.* Edited by John Francis Bannon. Norman: University of Oklahoma Press, 1954, pp. 288–98.

———, *Pageant in the Wilderness: The Story of the Escalante Expedition to the Interior Basin, 1776.* Salt Lake City: Utah State Historical Society, 1951. This was Bolton's last major work before his death and does not measure up to his other historical works. His "Historical Introduction" is almost a paraphrasing of the journal. It contains numerous errors. The subtitle of the book tends to downgrade the role of Father Domínguez in the enterprise.

Briggs, Walter. *Without Noise of Arms: The 1776 Domínguez-Escalante Search for a Route from Santa Fe to Monterey.* Flagstaff, Arizona: Northland Press, 1976.

Cerquone, Joseph. *In Behalf of Light: The Domínguez and Escalante Expedition of 1776.* Denver, Colorado: Bicentennial Expedition, Inc., 1976.

Crampton, C. Gregory. "The Discovery of the Green River." *Utah Historical Quarterly* 20 (1952): 299–312.

Harris, W. R. *The Catholic Church in Utah*. Salt Lake City, Utah, 1909. This contains the first English translation of the journal. It was made from a copy of the 1854 Mexican version and contains many errors.

Hill, Joseph J. "Spanish and Mexican Exploration and Trade Northwest from New Mexico into the Great Basin, 1765–1853." *Utah Historical Quarterly* 3 (1930): 3–23.

Maas, Otto. *Viajes de misionarios francescanos a la conquista del Neuvo Mexico*. Sevilla, Espana, 1915. Contains the journal from October 12, 1776, through January 3, 1777. It is based on the AGI, Guadalajara 516 copy.

Thomas, Alfred B. *Forgotten Frontiers: A Study of the Spanish Indian Policy of Don Juan Bautista de Anza, Governor of New Mexico, 1777-1787*. Norman: University of Oklahoma Press, 1932.

Tyler, S. Lyman, and Taylor, H. Darrel. "The Report of Fray Alonso de Posada in Relation to Quivera and Teguayo." *New Mexico Historical Review* 33 (1958): 285–314.

Tyler, S. Lyman. "The Spaniard and the Ute." *Utah Historical Quarterly* 22 (1954): 343–61.

Warner, Ted J. "The Significance of the Domínguez-Vélez de Escalante Expedition." In *Charles Redd Monographs in Western History: Essays on the American West, 1973–1974*, no. 5. Provo, Utah: Brigham Young University Press, 1975, 63–80.

Unpublished materials

Tyler, S. Lyman. "Before Escalante: An Early History of the Yuta Indians and the Area North of New Mexico." Ph.D. dissertation, University of Utah, 1951.